Reincarnation & KARMA

Reincarnation

& KARMA

By Edgar Cayce

A.R.E. Press
Since 1931

A.R.E. Press • Virginia Beach • Virginia

A.R.E. Press
215 67th Street
Virginia Beach, VA 23451–2061

Cayce, Edgar, 1877–1945.
   Reincarnation & karma / by Edgar Cayce
     p.   cm.
   ISBN 13: 978-0-87604-524-4 (trade pbk.)
   1. Reincarnation. 2. Karma. I. Title. II. Title: Reincarnation and karma.
   BL515.C375 2006
   133.901'35—dc22

                     2006015305

Cover design by Catherine Merchand

Contents

Foreword: Who Was Edgar Cayce? *by Charles Thomas Cayce* vii

An Explanation of the Cayce Readings *by John Van Auken* ix

Part 1   **Reincarnation** xiii

Chapter 1   Edgar Cayce's Discourses on Reincarnation 1

Chapter 2   Insightful Past-Life Readings by Edgar Cayce 25

Chapter 3   Planetary Sojourns: The Soul's Life Between
                  Incarnations 69

Chapter 4   Reincarnation Unnecessary: Breaking Free of the Wheel
                  of Karma and Reincarnation 94

Part 2   **Karma** 149

Chapter 5   Edgar Cayce's Discourses on Karma 151

Chapter 6   Examples of Karma in Edgar Cayce's Discourses 156

Chapter 7   Edgar Cayce's Tips for Meeting Karma 162

Chapter 8   From Karma to Grace 165

Foreword
Who Was Edgar Cayce?

It is a time in the earth when people everywhere seek to know more of the mysteries of the mind, the soul," said my grandfather, Edgar Cayce, from an unconscious trance from which he demonstrated a remarkable gift for clairvoyance.

His words are prophetic even today, as more and more Americans in these unsettled times are turning to psychic explanations for daily events. For example, according to a survey by the National Opinion Research Council nearly half of American adults believe they have been in contact with someone who has died, a figure twice that of ten years earlier. Two-thirds of all adults say they have had an ESP experience; ten years before that figure was only one-half.

Every culture throughout history has made note of its own members' gifted powers beyond the five senses. These rare individuals held special interest because they seemed able to provide solutions to life's pressing problems. America in the twenty-first century is no exception.

Edgar Cayce was perhaps the most famous and most carefully documented psychic of our time. He began to use his unusual abilities when he was a young man, and from then on for over forty years he would, usually twice a day, lie on a couch, go into a sleeplike state, and respond to questions. Over fourteen thousand of these discourses, called readings, were carefully transcribed by his secretary and preserved by the Edgar Cayce Foundation in Virginia Beach, Virginia. These psychic readings continue to provide inspiration, insight, and help with healing to tens of thousands of people.

Having only an eighth-grade education, Edgar Cayce lived a plain and simple life by the world's standards. As early as his childhood in Hopkinsville, Kentucky, however, he sensed that he had psychic ability. While alone one day he had a vision of a woman who told him he would have unusual power to help people. He also related experiences of "seeing" dead relatives. Once, while struggling with school lessons, he slept on his spelling book and awakened knowing the entire contents of the book.

As a young man he experimented with hypnosis to treat a recurring throat problem that caused him to lose his speech. He discovered that under hypnosis he could diagnose and describe treatments for the physical ailments of others, often without knowing or seeing the person with the ailment. People began to ask him other sorts of questions, and he found himself able to answer these as well.

In 1910 the *New York Times* published a two-page story with pictures about Edgar Cayce's psychic ability as described by a young physician, Wesley Ketchum, to a clinical research society in Boston. From that time on people from all over the country with every conceivable question sought his help.

In addition to his unusual talents, Cayce was a deeply religious man who taught Sunday school all of his adult life and read the entire Bible once for every year that he lived. He always tried to attune himself to God's will by studying the Scriptures and maintaining a rich prayer life, as well as by trying to be of service to those who came seeking help. He used his talents only for helpful purposes. Cayce's simplicity and humility and his commitment to doing good in the world continue to attract people to the story of his life and work and to the far-reaching information he gave.

Charles Thomas Cayce, Ph.D.
Executive Director
Association for Research and Enlightenment, Inc.

Editor's Explanation of Cayce's Discourses

Edgar Cayce dictated all of his discourses from a self-induced trance. A stenographer took his discourses down in shorthand and later typed them. Copies were sent to the person or persons who had requested the psychic reading, and one was put into the files of the organization, which built up around Cayce over the years, the Association for Research and Enlightenment (better known as the A.R.E.).

In his normal consciousness, Edgar Cayce spoke with a Southern accent but in the same manner as any other American. However, from the trance state, he spoke in the manner of the King James Bible, using "thees" and "thous." In trance, his syntax was also unusual. He put phrases, clauses, and sentences together in a manner that slows down any reader and requires careful attention in order to be sure of his meaning. This caused his stenographer to adopt some unusual punctuation in order to put into sentence form some of the long, complex thoughts conveyed by Cayce while in trance. Also, many of his discourses are so jam-packed with information and insights that it requires that one slow down and read more carefully in order to fully understand what he is intending.

From his trance state, Cayce explained that he got his information from two sources: (1) the inquiring individual's mind, mostly from his or her deeper, subconscious mind and (2) from the Universal Consciousness, the infinite mind within which the entire universe is conscious. He explained that every action and thought of every individual makes an impression upon the Universal Consciousness, an impression that can be psychically read. He correlated this with the Hindu concept of an Akashic Record, which is an ethereal, fourth-dimensional film upon which actions and thoughts are recorded and can be read at any time.

When giving one of his famous health readings, called physical readings, Cayce acted as if he were actually scanning the entire body of the person, from the inside out! He explained that the subconscious mind of everyone contains all of the data on the condition of the physical body it inhabits, and Cayce simply connected with the patient's deeper mind. He could also give the cause of the condition, even if it was from early childhood or from many lifetimes ago in a previous incarnation of the soul. This was knowable because the soul remembers all of its experiences. He explained that deeper portions of the subconscious mind are the mind of the soul, and portions of the subconscious and the soul are in the body with the personality.

In life readings and topic readings, Cayce also connected with the subconscious minds of those inquiring as well as the Universal Consciousness.

Occasionally, Cayce would not have the material being requested, and he would say, "We do not have that here." This implied that Cayce's mind was more directed than one might think. He was not open to everything. From trance, he explained that the suggestion given at the beginning of one of his psychic readings so directed his deeper mind and focused it on the task or subject requested that he truly did not have other topics available. However, on a few occasions, he seemed able to shift topics in the middle of a reading.

The typed readings have a standard format. Numbers were used in the place of the name of the person or persons receiving the reading, and a dash system kept track of how many readings the person had received. For example, reading 137-5 was the fifth reading for Mr. [137]. At the top of the reading are the reading number, the date and location, and the names or numbers (for privacy) of those in attendance. Occasionally the stenographer would include a note about other conditions, such as the presence of a manuscript that the in-trance Cayce was supposed to view psychically and comment on. In many cases, I left in the entire format of a recorded reading, but sometimes only a paragraph or two were pertinent to our study, and then I only give the reading number.

As I explained, Cayce dictated all of these discourses while he was in trance. In most cases, he spoke in a monotone voice. However, he would sometimes elevate his volume when saying a word or phrase. In these instances, his stenographer usually typed these words with all-capital letters, to give the reader some sense of Cayce's increased volume. These all-capital letters have been changed to italic typeface for readability, as well as emphasis. In many cases, these words appear to be rightly accentuated in Cayce's discourses. However, in some cases, it is not clear why he raised his voice.

Another style that the stenographer adopted was to capitalize all of the letters in Cayce's many affirmations (positive-thought or prayer-like passages to be used by the recipient as a tool for focusing and/or raising consciousness). I have also changed these to upper- and lower-case letters and italicized them. Questions asked Cayce have also been italicized for easier reference.

Whenever his stenographer was not sure if she had written down the correct word or thought that she might have missed or misunderstood a word, she inserted suggested words, comments, and explanations in [brackets]. If she knew of another reading that had similar material or that was being referred to during this reading, she would put the reading number in brackets. Cayce's entire collection of readings is available on CD-ROM from the A.R.E., so, even though the referenced reading may not be in this book, I left these references in for any future research; but several of the readings that have references are in this book. Within the text of a reading, all (parentheses) are asides made by Cayce himself while in trance, not by his stenographer. She only used [brackets] within the text of a reading. In the preliminary material, she used parentheses in the normal manner. My comments are indicated by the term "Editor's Note."

A few common abbreviations use in these discourses were: "GD' for Gladys Davis, the primary stenographer; "GC" for Gertrude Cayce, Edgar's wife and the predominant conductor of the readings, and 'EC" for Edgar Cayce.

—John Van Auken, Editor

Part 1

Reincarnation

1

●

Edgar Cayce's Discourses on Reincarnation

Text of Reading 5753-1

This psychic reading was given by Edgar Cayce at his home, on the 16th day of June 1933, before the Second Annual Congress of the Association for Research and Enlightenment, Inc., in accordance with request by those present.

P R E S E N T

Edgar Cayce; Gertrude Cayce, Conductor; Gladys Davis, Steno. And approximately thirty-five other people attending the Congress.

R E A D I N G

Time of Reading 5:00 to 6:00 P.M.

GC: You will give at this time a comprehensive discourse on reincarnation. If the soul returns to the earth through a succession of appearances, you will explain why this is necessary or desirable and will clarify through explanation the laws governing such returns. You will answer the questions, which will be asked on this subject.

EC: Yes. In giving even an approach to the subject sought here, it is well that there be given some things that may be accepted as standards from which conclusions—or where parallels—may be drawn, that there may be gathered in the minds of those who would approach same some understanding, some concrete examples, that may be applied in their own individual experience.

Each soul that enters, then, must have had an impetus from some beginning that is of the Creative Energy, or of a first cause.

What, then, was—or is—the first cause; for if there be law pertaining to the first cause it must be an unchangeable law, and is—is—as "I AM that I am!" For this is the basis from which one would reason:

The first cause was, that the created would be the companion for the Creator; that it, the creature, would—through its manifestations in the activity of that given unto the creature—show itself to be not only worthy of, but companionable to, the Creator.

Hence, every form of life that man sees in a material world is an essence or manifestation of the Creator; not the Creator, but a manifestation of a first cause—and in its own sphere, its own consciousness of its activity in that plane or sphere.

Hence, as man in this material world passes through, there are the manifestations of the attributes that the consciousness attributes to, or finds coinciding with, that activity which is manifested; hence becomes then as the very principle of the law that would govern an entrance into a manifestation.

Then a soul, the offspring of a Creator, entering into a consciousness that became a manifestation in any plane or sphere of activity, given that free-will for its use of those abilities, qualities, conditions in its experience, demonstrates, manifests, shows forth, that it reflects in its activity towards that first cause.

Hence in the various spheres that man sees (that are demonstrated, manifested, in and before self) even in a material world, all forces, all activities, are a manifestation. Then, that which would be the companionable, the at-oneness with, the ability to be one with, becomes necessary for the demonstration or manifestation of those attributes in and through all force, all demonstration, in a sphere.

Because an atom, a matter, a form, is changed does not mean that the essence, the source or the spirit of it has changed; only in its form of manifestation, and *not* in its relation with the first cause. That man reaches that consciousness in the material plane of being aware of what he does about or with the consciousness of the knowledge, the intelligence, the first cause, makes or produces that which is known as the entering into the first cause, principles, basis, or the essences, that there may be demonstrated in that manifested that which gains for the soul, for the entity, that which would make the soul an acceptable companion to the Creative Force, Creative Influence. See?

As to how, where, when, and what produces the entrance into a material manifestation of an entity, a soul:

In the beginning was that which set in motion that which is seen in manifested form with the laws governing same. The inability of destroying matter, the ability of each force, each source of power or contact—as it meets in its various forms, produces that which is a manifestation in a particular sphere. This may be seen in those elements used in the various manifested ways of preparing for man, in many ways, those things that bespeak of the laws that govern man's relationship to the first cause, or God.

Then, this is the principle:

Like begets like. Those things that are positive and negative forces combine to form in a different source, or different manifestation, the combinations of which each element, each first principle manifested, has gained from its associations—in its activities—that which has been brought to bear by self or that about it, to produce that manifestation.

Hence man, the crowning of all manifestations in a material world—a causation world, finds self as the cause and the product of that he (man), with those abilities given, has been able to produce, or demonstrate, or manifest from that he (the soul) has gained, does gain, in the transition, the change, the going toward that (and being of that) from which he came.

Periods, times, places: That which is builded, each in its place, each in its time.

This is shown to man in the elemental world about him. Man's consciousness of that about him is gained through that he, man, does about the knowledge of that he is, as in relation to that from which he came and towards which he is going.

Hence, in man's analysis and understanding of himself, it is as well to know from whence he came as to know whither he is going.

Ready for questions.

Q: What is meant by inequality of experience? Is it a strong argument for reincarnation?

A: Considering that which has just been presented, isn't it the same argument?

Q: Is experience limited to this earth plane?

A: As each entity, each soul, in the various consciousnesses, passes from one to another, it—the soul—becomes conscious of that about self in that sphere—to which it, the entity, the soul attains in a materially manifested way or manner.

Hence the entity develops *through* the varied spheres of the earth and its solar system, and the companions of varied experiences in that solar system, or spheres of development or activity; as in some ways accredited correctly to the planetary influences in an experience. The entity develops *through* those varied spheres.

Hence the sun, the moon, the stars, the position in the heavens or in all of the hosts of the solar systems that the earth occupies—all have their influence in the same manner (this is a very crude illustration, but very demonstrative) that the effect of a large amount of any element would attract a compass. Drawn to! Why? Because of the influence of which the mind element of a soul, an entity, has become conscious!

A soul, an entity, is as real as a physical entity, and is as subject to laws as the physical body as subject to the laws in a material world and the elements thereof!

Does fire burn the soul or the physical body?

Yet, self may cast self into a fire element by doing that the soul knows to be wrong!

What would make a wrong and a right? A comparison of that the soul knows its consciousness to be in accord or contrariwise with, in relation to that which gave it existence.

Q: Are not transferred memories misappropriated by individuals and considered to be personal experiences?

A: Personal experiences have their influence upon the inner soul, while disincarnate entities (that may be earth-bound, or that may be heaven-bound) may influence the thought of an entity or a mind.

But, who gives the law to have an element to influence, whether from self or from others? That same as from the beginning. The *will* of the soul that it may be one with the first cause.

In the material, the mental, and the spiritual experience of many souls, many entities, it has been found that there *be* those influences that *do* have their effect upon the thought of those that would do this or that. Who gives it? Self!

Just as it is when an entity, a body, fills its mind (mentally, materially) with those experiences that bespeak of those things that add to the carnal forces of an experience. Just so does the mind become the builder throughout. And the mental mind, or physical mind, becomes *carnally* directed!

The mind is the builder ever, whether in the spirit or in the flesh. If one's mind is filled with those things that bespeak of the spirit, that one becomes spiritual-minded.

As we may find in a material world: Envy, strife, selfishness, greediness, avarice, are the children of *man*! Longsuffering, kindness, brotherly love, good deeds, are the children of the spirit of light.

Choose ye (as it has ever been given) whom ye will serve.

This is not beggaring the question! As individuals become abased, or possessed, are their thoughts guided by those in the borderland? Certainly! If allowed to be!

But he that looks within is higher, for the spirit knoweth the Spirit of its Maker—and the children of same are as given. And, "My Spirit beareth witness with thy spirit," saith He that giveth life!

What *is* Life? A manifestation of the first cause—God!

Q: Explain, in the light of reincarnation, the cycle of development towards maturity in individuals.

A: As an individual in any experience, in any period, uses that of which it (the soul or entity) is conscious in relation to the laws of the Creative Forces, so does that soul, that entity, develop towards—what? A companionship with the Creative influence!

Hence karma, to those disobeying—by making for self that which would be as the towers of Babel, or as the city of Gomorrah, or as the fleshpots of Egypt, or as the caring for those influences in the experience that satisfy or gratify self without thought of the effect upon that which it has in its own relation to the first cause! Hence to many this becomes as the stumblingblock.

It is as was given by Him, "I am the way. No man approaches the Father but by me." But, does a soul crucify the flesh even as He, when it finds within itself that it must work out its own salvation in a material world, by entering and re-entering that there may be made manifest that consciousness in the soul that would make it a companion with the Creator?

Rather is the law of forgiveness made of effect in thine experience, through Him that would stand in thy stead; for He is the way, that light ever ready to aid when there is the call upon—and the trust of the soul in—that first cause!

Has it not been given that there *is* an influence in the mind, the thought of man, from the outside? Then, would those that have lost their way become the guides and both fall in the ditch? Or would the soul trust in the Way, and the Light, and seek in that way that there may be shown the light?

What caused the first influences in the earth that brought selfishness? The desire to be as gods, in that rebellion became the order of the mental forces in the soul; and sin entered.

Q: *What is the strongest argument against reincarnation?*

A: That there is the law of cause and effect in *material* things. But the strongest argument against reincarnation is also, turned over, the strongest argument for it; as in *any* principle, when reduced to its essence. For the *law* is set—and it happens! Though a soul may will itself *never* to reincarnate, but must burn and burn and burn—or suffer and suffer and suffer! For, the heaven and hell is built by the soul! The companionship in God is being one with Him; and the gift of God is being conscious of being one with Him, yet apart from Him—or one with, yet apart from, the Whole.

Q: *What is the strongest argument for reincarnation?*

A: Just as given. Just turn it over; or, as we have outlined.

We are through for the present.

Text of Reading 5749-14

This Psychic Reading given by Edgar Cayce at the office of the Association, Arctic Crescent, Virginia Beach, Va., this 14th day of May, 1941, in accordance with request made by the self—Mr. Thomas Sugrue, Active Member of the Ass'n for Research & Enlightenment, Inc.

PRESENT

Edgar Cayce; Hugh Lynn Cayce, Conductor; Gladys Davis, Steno. Thomas Sugrue and Gertrude Cayce.

READING

Time of Reading 4:10 to 4:35 P.M. Eastern Standard Time.

HLC: You will have before you the enquiring mind of the entity, Thomas Sugrue, present in this room, and certain of the problems which confront him in composing the manuscript of *There Is a River*.

The entity is now ready to describe the philosophical concepts, which have been given through this source, and wishes to parallel and align them with known religious tenets, especially those of Christian theology.

The entity does not wish to set forth a system of thought, nor imply that all questions of a philosophical nature can be answered through this source—the limitations of the finite mind prevent this.

But the entity wishes to answer those questions, which will naturally arise in the mind of the reader, and many of the questions, which are being asked by all people in the world today.

Therefore the entity presents certain problems and questions, which you will answer as befits the entity's understanding and the task of interpretation before him.

EC: Yes, we have the enquiring mind, Thomas Sugrue, and those problems, those questions that arise in the mind of the entity at this period. Ready for questions.

Q: The first problem concerns the reason for creation. Should this be given as God's desire to experience Himself, God's desire for companionship, God's desire for expression, or in some other way?

A: God's desire for companionship and expression.

Q: The second problem concerns that which is variously called evil, darkness, negation, sin. Should it be said that this condition existed as a necessary element of creation, and the soul, given free will, found itself with the power to indulge in it, or lose itself in it? Or should it be said that this is a condition created by the activity of the soul itself? Should it be described, in either case, as a state of consciousness, a gradual lack of awareness of self and self's relation to God?

A: It is the free will and it's losing itself in its relationship to God.

Q: The third problem has to do with the fall of man. Should this be described as something, which was inevitable in the destiny of souls, or something which God did not desire, but which He did not prevent once He had given free will? The problem here is to reconcile the omniscience of God and His knowledge of all things with the free will of the soul and the soul's fall from grace.

A: He did not prevent, once having given free will. For, He made the individual entities or souls in the beginning. For, the beginnings of sin, of course, were in seeking expression of themselves outside of the plan or the way in which God had expressed same. Thus it was the individual, see?

Having given free will, then—though having the foreknowledge, though being omnipotent and omnipresent—it is only when the soul that is a portion of God *chooses* that God knows the end thereof.

Q: The fourth problem concerns man's tenancy on earth. Was it originally intended that souls remain out of earthly forms, and were the races originated as a necessity resulting from error?

A: The earth and its manifestations were only the expression of God and not necessarily as a place of tenancy for the souls of men, until man was created—to meet the needs of existing conditions.

Q: The fifth problem concerns an explanation of the Life Readings. From a study of these it seems that there is a trend downward, from early incarnations, toward greater earthliness and less mentality. Then there is a swing upward, accompanied by suffering, patience, and understanding. Is this the normal pattern, which results in virtue and oneness with God obtained by free will and mind?

A: This is correct. It is the pattern as it is set in Him.

Q: The sixth problem concerns interplanetary and inter-system dwelling, between earthly lives. It was given through this source that the entity Edgar Cayce, after the experience as Uhjltd, went to the system of Arcturus, and then returned to earth. Does this indicate a usual or an unusual step in soul evolution?

A: As indicated, or as has been indicated in other sources besides this as respecting this very problem—Arcturus is that which may be called the center of this universe, through which individuals pass and at which period there comes the choice of the individual as to whether it is to return to complete there—that is, in this planetary system, our sun, the earth sun and its planetary system—or to pass on to others. This was an unusual step, and yet a usual one.

Q: *The seventh problem concerns implications from the sixth problem. Is it necessary to finish the solar system cycle before going to other systems?*

A: Necessary to finish the solar cycle.

Q: *Can oneness be attained—or the finish of evolution reached—on any system, or must it be in a particular one?*

A: Depending upon what system the entity has entered, to be sure. It may be completed in any of the many systems.

Q: *Must the solar cycle be finished on earth, or can it be completed on another planet, or does each planet have a cycle of its own which must be finished?*

A: If it is begun on the earth it must be finished on the earth. The solar system of which the earth is a part is only a portion of the whole. For, as indicated in the number of planets about the earth, they are of one and the same—and they are relative one to another. It is the cycle of the whole system that is finished, see?

Q: *The eighth problem concerns the pattern made by parents at conception. Should it be said that this pattern attracts a certain soul because it approximates conditions, which that soul wishes to work with?*

A: It approximates conditions. It does not set. For, the individual entity or soul, given the opportunity, has its own free will to work in or out of those problems as presented by that very union. Yet the very union, of course, attracts or brings a channel or an opportunity for the expression of an individual entity.

Q: *Does the incoming soul take on of necessity some of the parents' karma?*

A: Because of its relative relationship to same, yes. Otherwise, no.

Q: *Does the soul itself have an earthly pattern, which fits back into the one created by the parents?*

A: Just as indicated, it is relative—as one related to another; and because of the union of activities they are brought in the pattern. For in such there is the explanation of universal or divine laws, which are ever one and the same; as indicated in the expression that God moved within Himself and then He didn't change, though did bring to Himself that of His own being made crucified even in the flesh.

Q: Are there several patterns which a soul might take on, depending on what phase of development it wished to work upon—i.e., could a soul choose to be one of several personalities, any of which would fit its individuality?

A: Correct.

Q: Is the average fulfillment of the soul's expectation more or less than fifty percent?

A: It's a continuous advancement, so it is more than fifty percent.

Q: Are hereditary, environment and will equal factors in aiding or retarding the entity's development?

A: Will is the greater factor, for it may overcome any or all of the others; provided that will is made one with the pattern, see? For, no influence of heredity, environment or what not, surpasses the will; else why would there have been that pattern shown in which the individual soul, no matter how far astray it may have gone, may enter with Him into the holy of holies?

Q: The ninth problem concerns the proper symbols, or similes, for the Master, the Christ. Should Jesus be described as the soul who first went through the cycle of earthly lives to attain perfection, including perfection in the planetary lives also?

A: He should be. This is as the man, see?

Q: Should this be described as a voluntary mission One Who was already perfected and returned to God, having accomplished His Oneness in other planes and systems?

A: Correct.

Q: Should the Christ Consciousness be described as the awareness within each soul, imprinted in pattern on the mind and waiting to be awakened by the will, of the soul's oneness with God?

A: Correct. That's the idea exactly!

Q: Please list the names of the incarnations of the Christ, and of Jesus, indicating where the development of the man Jesus began.

A: First, in the beginning, of course; and then as Enoch, Melchizedek, in the perfection. Then in the earth of Joseph, Joshua, Jeshua, Jesus.

Q: The tenth problem concerns the factors of soul evolution. Should mind, the builder, be described as the last development because it should not unfold until it has a firm foundation of emotional virtues?

A: This might be answered Yes and No, both. But if it is presented in that there is kept, willfully, see, that desire to be in the at-onement, then it is necessary for that attainment before it recognizes mind as the way.

Q: *The eleventh problem concerns a parallel with Christianity. Is Gnosticism the closest type of Christianity to that which is given through this source?*

A: This is a parallel, and was the commonly accepted one until there began to be set rules in which there were the attempts to take short cuts. And there are none in Christianity!

Q: *What action of the early church, or council, can be mentioned as that which ruled reincarnation from Christian theology?*

A: Just as indicated—the attempts of individuals to accept or take advantage of, because of this knowledge, see?

Q: *Do souls become entangled in other systems as they did in this system?*

A: In other systems that represent the same as the earth does in this system, yes.

Q: *Is there any other advice which may be given to this entity at this time in the preparation of these chapters?*

A: Hold fast to that ideal, and using Him ever as the Ideal. And hold up that *necessity* for each to meet the same problems. And *do not* attempt to shed or to surpass or go around the Cross. *This* is that upon which each and every soul *must* look and know it is to be borne in self *with* Him.

We are through for the present.

Text of Reading 900-70 M 30
(Stockbroker, Jewish)

This Psychic Reading given by Edgar Cayce at his office, 322 Grafton Avenue, Dayton, Ohio, this 12th day of May, 1925, in accordance with request made by [900].

PRESENT

Edgar Cayce; Mrs. Cayce, Conductor; Gladys Davis, Steno.

READING

Time of Reading 11:00 A.M. Dayton Savings Time.

GC: You will have before you the subject matter as was given in psychic state by the body Edgar Cayce, and questions on same as prepared by the enquiring mind of [900]. You will answer these questions as I ask them, in such a manner as to be understood by the mind of [900].

EC: Yes, we have this here. We have had this before, you see, that as transcribed from that given by Edgar Cayce while in the psychic state. Ready for questions.

Q: *Explain as clearly as possible the definition of Evolution as relates to Man, first in Spirit plane, then in flesh and blood on earth and again in spirit plane. What is man and how may we in flesh become fully conscious and aware of the Spiritual Self?*

A: In this we find the understanding would, from physical viewpoint, never be understood by the cycle as is asked. The evolution of man in spiritual plane being one, the evolution of man in flesh being another. Hence, as has been given, hard to understand conditions in one plane when viewed from another plane, without the realization of having experienced that plane. Now evolution in flesh, as is seen, is the passing through the flesh plane and in the various experiences of man's sojourn in earth, through his (man's) environment as created and made by man, this is called man's evolution in the earth plane. As we have in the beginning of man's sojourn in earth plane, we find under what is termed at the present time or day, or plane of man, the primitive man. The man seeking the first of the attributes of fleshly existence, known only by those conditions surrounding man and his environments. As man applies the laws of which he (man) becomes conscious of, the development of man brings forth those results merited by that knowledge. As man passes into the spiritual plane from earthly existence, the development in the spiritual plane becoming the same evolution in spiritual planes as is acquired in the physical plane, and until man becomes in the spiritual sense the one-ness with the Creator's forces, as is set by example of the Son of Man coming in the flesh to the earth plane to manifest in the flesh the will made one with the Father, passing through the physical plane, passing through the spiritual planes, making *all* one with the Father. This we find then is evolution. Man's development through man's acquiring man's understanding of spiritual laws, of earthly laws, of God's laws, and applying same in the earth. Then truly is it given, "The righteous shall inherit the earth."

Q: Does Man created as Matter, Force and Mind mean Physical, Spiritual and Mental?

A: Man created having the attributes of the physical, the spiritual, the mental, to work with in his own development. These, as it were, tools of the whole man, the all being then one, and that same separated is the attributes of the various conditions, each having its single, its separate attributes, and man using same for man's development.

Q: When earth plane became ready for Man, how did he first get here? In the Bible we have the story of Adam and Eve. Explain in a reasonable, logical way how did Man first appear on earth. Explain this in relation to birth, to conception.

A: As is given, man, when earth became habitable for physical man, man entered in the plane, just as the highest of created forces in the earth plane. Then became man amenable to laws of earth plane, and amenable to physical birth, physical conditions, physical conceptions, physical forces as applied to the whole man. Physical, mental and spiritual forces manifest in man, taken in this conception as was given from the beginning. As the earth plane became in that state wherein man may find residence, the spirit forces as are developing through the spiritual forces to make one with the Father, given the soul of man to make manifest in the flesh. All souls were created in the beginning, all spirit of one spirit, Spirit of God, that spirit manifest in flesh, that spirit manifest in all creation, whether of earthly forces or Universal forces, all spirit being one spirit. All flesh not one flesh. Flesh being that as has merited by its development in its plane of existence.

Q: Is every chemical quality found in the animal, vegetable and mineral kingdom of the world found in Man? Explain, if not, what is meant by "There is found in Living Man all of that that may be found without in the whole world".

A: All those essential forces as are manifest in the Universe are manifest in the living man, and above that the soul of man. The chemical or material, or animated forces as are seen in all animal, vegetable, mineral forces, with their combinations, are found in the combinations in man, and from same may be created, for man is Lord over creation, from the physical viewpoint.

Q: Explain how the example of Man's developing and improving his mode of living scientifically on earth, for example in medical work and all other sciences, proves his development and evolution on earth and other planes.

A: Man's development, as given, is of man's understanding and applying the laws of the Universe, and as man applies those, man develops, man brings up the whole generation of man. Individuals we find carry out certain elements and laws, and gradually man becomes capable of applying and using those in the everyday life of man. This, whether applied in medical science, in anatomal [anatomic] science, in mechanical science or what not, is merely the development, or the application as man applies to Universal laws as are ever, and have ever been, existent in the Universe. As is in this. That producing electrical units of force was just as applicable to the Universal forces in the days of Adam as in the days of the Master, or as in the days of today. Those laws applying to aerial of transmission just as applicable in one as in other. Man not understanding those. Many times has the evolution of the earth reached the stage of development as it has today and then sank again, to rise again in the next development. Some along one line, some along others, for often we find the higher branches of so-called learning destroys itself in the seed it produces in man's development, as we have in medical forces, as we have astrological forces, as we have in some forms of spiritual forces, as we have in forms of destructive forces of the various natures.

Q: *Explain how the Law of Relativity applies to Man's development to his evolution?*

A: As each and every atom in the Universe has its relative relation with every other atom, then man's development lies in the relativity of all forces, whether applied in the physical world as existent today, or that existence in man's earthly existence before, for the relativity of one force applies to another. Hence all relative forces apply to man's development, whether mental, physical or spiritual.

Q: *To what development must the soul reach before it may first find lodgment in the flesh?*

A: Desire for flesh.

Q: *How does Soul manifest Will's desire to take on fleshly existence?*

A: Spiritual subject and spiritually understood. When we reach those conditions and that development necessary to understand the law of taking those, we may gather these forces.

Q: *Explain: Reincarnation of the Soul from an appearance in Flesh to the next as it relates to Evolution, and step by step tell us just what other body the soul and spirit takes on after it leaves flesh existence and of what the soul and spirit becomes conscious after it leaves flesh existence.*

A: We are through.

Reading 5749-3

Q: *Discuss the various phases of spiritual development before and after reincarnation in the earth.*

A: This may be illustrated best in that which has been sought through example in the earth.

When there was in the beginning a man's advent into the plane known as earth, and it became a living soul, amenable to the laws that govern the plane itself as presented, the Son of man entered earth as the first man. Hence the Son of man, the Son of God, the Son of the first Cause, making manifest in a material body.

This was not the first spiritual influence, spiritual body, spiritual manifestation in the earth, but the first man—flesh and blood; the first carnal house, the first amenable body to the laws of the plane in its position in the universe.

For, the earth is only an atom in the universe of worlds!

And man's development began through the laws of the generations in the earth; thus the development, retardment, or the alterations in those positions in a material plane.

And with error entered that as called *death*, which is only a transition—or through God's other door—into that realm where the entity has builded, in its manifestations as related to the knowledge and activity respecting the law of the universal influence.

Hence the development is through the planes of experience that an entity may become one *with* the first cause; even as the angels that wait before the Throne bring the access of the influence in the experience through the desires and activities of an entity, or being, in whatever state, place or plane of development the entity is passing.

For, in the comprehension of no time, no space, no beginning, no end, there may be the glimpse of what simple transition or birth into the material is; as passing through the other door into another consciousness.

Death in the material plane is passing through the outer door into a consciousness in the material activities that partakes of what the entity, or soul, has done with its spiritual truth in its manifestations in the other sphere.

Hence, as there came the development of that first entity of flesh and blood through the earth plane, he became *indeed* the Son—through the things which He experienced in the varied planes, as the development came to the oneness with the position in that which man terms the Triune.

Q: Are angels and archangels synonymous with that which we call the laws of the universe? If so, explain and give an example.

A: They are as the laws of the universe; as is Michael the lord of the Way, *not* the Way but the lord of the Way, hence disputed with the influence of evil as to the way of the spirit of the teacher or director in his entrance through the outer door. [See Jude 1:9 in re Michael the archangel "when contending with the devil about the body of Moses" when Moses died.]

Q: Describe some of the planes into which entities pass on experiencing the change called death.

A: Passing from the material consciousness to a spiritual or cosmic, or outer consciousness, oft does an entity or being not become conscious of that about it; much in the same manner as an entity born into the material plane only becomes conscious gradually of that designated as time and space for the material or third dimensional plane. In the passage the entity becomes conscious, or the recognition of being in a fourth or higher dimensional plane takes place, much in the same way as the consciousness is gained in the material.

For, as we have given, that we see manifested in the material plane is but a shadow of that in the spiritual plane.

In materiality we find some advance faster, some grow stronger, some become weaklings. Until there is redemption through the acceptance of the law (or love of God, as manifested through the Channel or the Way), there can be little or no development in a material or spiritual plane. But all must pass under the rod, even as He—who entered into materiality.

We are through.

Editor's Note: The following Cayce discourses on reincarnation begin with a request to interpret a dream concerning reincarnation.

Text of Reading 900-156 M 30
(Stockbroker, Jewish)

This Psychic Reading given by Edgar Cayce at his office, 115 West 35th Street, Virginia Beach, Va., this 4th day of November, 1925, in accordance with request made by self—[900].

P R E S E N T

Edgar Cayce; Mrs. Cayce, Conductor; Gladys Davis, Steno.

R E A D I N G

Time of Reading 11:20 A.M. Eastern Standard Time. New York City.

GC: You will have before you the body and the enquiring mind of [900], of Apt. . . . , . . . St., New York City, and the dreams this body had on the dates which I will give you. You will give the interpretation and lesson to be gained from each of these, as I read same to you, and you will answer the questions which I shall ask you regarding same.

EC: Yes, we have the body, the enquiring mind, [900]. This we have had here before. The dreams, as we see, are the conditions in subconscious, mental, superconscious and cosmic forces, weighed together in such a manner as to give to the body–mind consciousness those of lessons or of visions of conditions, whether in the mental, the superficial, the subconscious or from the cosmic forces, and often are a combination of all, for as has been given, there may be much given as relating to dreams, and especially when one has reached that development such as this entity, and when there is such a message to be given to the peoples, that the living forces as manifest in the physical world may be known of men, through the study of that phenomena as is experienced and known by this entity. Ready for dreams.

Q: *Wednesday morning, Oct. 28, at home . . . Wednesday night while reading Bible: "Saw an old man—or one with iron gray hair walk by me."*

A: This, as the subconscious and mental, gives to the consciousness that understanding as is seen by the entity, for as to the physical mind, one of ripe years in earth plane, one with mental and physical experiences that have given the physical mind that understanding, that concept, of the physical existences in the plane of those conditions necessary to make knowledge. Such is being acquired by this entity, and in the emblematical form is shown the lesson. Seek then the knowledge of the seer and the sages, that through this entity much may be given to a waiting world.

Q: *Thursday Morning, Oct. 29. "Numbers 119."*

A: This, as we see, the physical mind attempting to gain from the subconscious forces that knowledge of conditions pertaining to that that is paramount in the physical mind. Relating, then, to that condition which will arise, as has been given, regarding prices of stocks—L & N, see? This, as we have seen, will occur when other changes have set in and the combinations begin to break up.

Q: *Does this 119 refer to L & N or Southern?*

A: As given, this will occur as a price of L & N, but as given in those concerning the combinations and changes that will come in the future.

Q: *The whole of this dream not remembered by [900]. Recall and interpret. That recalled as follows: "I was married to Miriam Miller and things seemed miserable or wrong. Some certain things seemed unsatisfactory, but it was within myself as well as circumstances."*

A: The portion not recalled is as this: There was the meeting of a certain board and the entity, with others, especially with one, Wormser, was present. The question as to the relations with an individual was brought up in a manner that entity felt that the reference was to self. Then that remembered brought that to the remembrance, or to the body consciousness, in the form as given, for this then represents in the physical mind a condition not wholly acceptable or pleasing to the entity, as to duty to self and to others. Then the lesson should be, as the warnings have been given to entity that there is the duty to self, to home ties, to that of the social ties, to that of business relations and business social connections, these all must be made into that oneness of purpose; that is, to give best in self to service to each and all of these conditions as they arise, see?

Q: *What reference has this in my present life?*

A: That as given.

Q: *Does this indicate just a condition I have overcome—indicating in emblematical form the overcoming in the flesh and the blessings therefrom—or the submission to the flesh test and the dissatisfaction therefrom?*

A: Rather the combination of each as is given, see? bringing in the mental forces of entity, then, the not entire satisfactory condition, see? yet each duty must be weighed, considered and kept in that *one purpose* manner, service to self, to man, to social ties, to all those conditions as given.

Q: *Does it also show me that reason of the phenomenized condition—to strengthen and test the individual portion, that under every condition the Spiritual Power in the portion is used in the manner the Power of the Whole is used? In this do I see my own development?*

A: In this entity sees own development, with the weaknesses, with the strengths as gained for self and conditions as existent, as given, see?

Q: *"I was back in a department store, a clerk behind the counter, even as I was in past days. I waited on people—serving them, but it seemed I was in love with some girl. Some dissatisfaction resulted and I was miserable. Then the Voice: 'Here are you tested as much as anywhere.' Then I felt terrible, as though I had failed in something, in living up to that which was expected of me—that I had retarded—returned to old conditions, instead of living the ideals I had set for myself."*

A: Rather that in this as the interpretation and lesson: That often the self, mentally, spiritually, physically, should take stock of self, as is seen in department stores run on the correct basis, and that the loves for certain or for particular conditions that exist in the life, whether the mental or the desire of flesh, or of the spiritual forces, all must be weighed well, and as the Voice is given, the test is that entity keeps the standard in that manner that gives the progressive forces to self and abilities to give out in service, as is necessary for advancement in every phase of the phenomenized life, see?

Q: *Does this refer to [136] in any way, in my failure to live up to the test in relation to her—that is the test of being in the flesh what God is in the Spiritual, that I may attain that Spiritual condition—and being this in the flesh in every condition of life—every phase?*

A: This rather that of self than of relations with others, save that as is given, see?

Q: Explain this particular reference of failure to so exemplify the perfection of the Whole in the individual phenomenized form—that is the secret of the whole message—"That The Individual Phenomenized Being, possessing all the Elements of the Whole, shall in phenomenized form manifest the Perfection of the Elemental Whole—thus proving Christ—proving Itself ready for the Work, Power, Action, Peace and Eternal Life One with the Whole—ready for the Kingdom of God." This is the kernel of the whole message of [900] is it not? Where or in what phenomenized relation of life is [900] not measuring up to this test?

A: In only that manner as is given, see? All of these, when measured by that as given in the mind of [900] as necessary for the readiness to present that force as draws men closer to the Kingdom, see? Then measure the standard—not measure self by self, but as to the standard set in the *one* as *exemplifies God* in the *flesh.*

Q: The subconscious—cosmic consciousness—super-consciousness—spiritual forces, which reflect in symbolic form in our physical life. Correct?

A: Correct.

Q: Let the light represent the Spiritual, the film the physical faculties of senses (mind), and the moving picture on the screen this physical life—talking, feeling, tasting, thinking, emotion, etc., and one has a good comparison. Changing pictures, but One Fixed Light.

A: Correct.

Q: Explain this phenomena shown to [900] objectively and co-relate with Edgar Cayce in psychic state and with dreams and voice heard when asleep by [900].

A: As is seen, and as may be given in the physical, as has been explained before. One, Edgar Cayce, working from within, see? [900] working from the objective forces, yet gaining from within the resounding, or the re-projection through voice, through dream, through the co-relation of all of these faculties that are guided by spiritual forces from within, while that as is obtained through Edgar Cayce guided by that from without, through another force than self, see?

Q: "Saw numbers 127 and others higher but can't remember. Recall, interpret, co-relate and explain how they should be used."

A: This as already given, relating to the L & N in its advance, and is given that the entity, [900], may begin to understand numbers in their co-relation one with another, see?

Q: Sunday Night, Nov. 1, 1925, at home, while reading Isis Unveiled by H. P.

Blavatsky. "Dozing over that part of the book regarding Reincarnation, the follow-ing: Saw a book case with a glass door of which the glass was cracked. The Voice: 'We have drapes to cover that here.'"

A: This, as we find, the mind of the individual, [900], co-relating with subconscious and with cosmic forces those portions of truths gathered in that just read. This, then, presented as bookcase, as knowledge—cov-ered, see? As conditions show break, the film over same, the presenta-tion of the various conditions, shows how these must be studied by the entity and gained in a way that the entity will bring the perfect under-standing to self concerning, relating to, that phase of the conditions not yet understood by many, for this, as we see, turns to the phenomenized conditions as are existent in the earth's plane, and through the study of same will the entity gain the knowledge pertaining to reincarnation and its effect on the lives, on the conditions existent in the earth's plane.

Q: Does this indicate I am to get for myself, from my own experience the knowl-edge of reincarnation?

A: This, as given, the entity will gain this conception for self of the phenomenized forces of reincarnation in the earth's plane.

Q: Is indicated that I should give my version—my own understanding in my own simple way—for although I understand what is meant, I don't understand the theo-sophical terminology. Give then simply, in my simple way (use phenomena of gas for example) for all minds to grasp, rather than just students of theosophy or any one branch of study. Is that what is meant?

A: That is what is meant, for as we see, we may use that terminology from gas; from the whole there arises that power, that force, in another form to work wonders in the various mechanical devices made by man, see? Power of an individual object (if choose to be termed so) giving of self in another form, yet that same form. Same may be applicable from the terminology of the electrical unit. As the force and power of the turbine is manifested in its rotation, the same is given off in many chan-nels, for the electrical units, which may be added to or taken from, to give service to man. Or as may be termed in the vegetable kingdom, a grain of wheat is sown. It dies, that the fruit of same may germinate into other fruit, see? The same Spirit—not the same Body, yet with all the potential faculties of reproduction within itself and of the ability to supply food in the same proportion, dependent upon its environment throughout its fruition, same as man, as man passes through one environment gaining that knowledge, that force necessary for the body-mind, the spiritual forces, pertaining to the physical conditions as manifest in same, see? Then the spiritual elements of same gaining in the phenomenized form in a world those things necessary to make the entity One with the Whole, see? All of these, then, may be co-related, may be brought under one head, one phraseology, one terminology, by the mental forces and abilities of [900], and given in the simple form and manner to the public, the world, that they may understand that these forces ever manifest their God's spiritual forces in the world, manifesting through the same entity—spiritually.

We are through for the present.

Editor's Note: The same dreamer got the following reading from Cayce on a different reincarnation dream.

Reading 900-273

Q: This morning, or this morning's dream had regarding reincarnation, the details of which are here written.

A: In this there are presented the fundamentals, as it were, of many various experiences as the entity will pass through by the concerted effort of the body conscious mind, for in the presentation of the vision as is seen, these become those properties of the physical mind, obtained from a vision, as it were, of the various forces as are loosed in the Universal Forces by disintegration, and by re-integration, as it were, of various forces manifesting individually and collectively, and as these various forces are presented, we will find the various phases of re-incarnation, its fundamentals, its application to that of the various conditions as present themselves to man, in the developing of the mental abilities of man to understand conditions as are seen in the world today—for, as we see presented here an individual well in years, yet just presenting the first phases of a renewed *life*, and then we see the same phases as are termed by *individuals* know to the *entity*, and changed again into realities by the presentation of various forms of an intelligent force, acting dependently, yet independent in their reaction, see? meaning as in this: That, as each force in the reincarnation of the elements begin as in this—in creation, see—now we are beginning from first principles, see? from the first principles, we find these are separated into integral parts. For instance, as we take that as the most elemental conditions—water— separated into two elements, yet each time these elements are combined in certain forms the same common principle is presented. Now, we have had, then, the reincarnation of an elemental principle into that as is materialized before the *material* forces in earth's plane into the form of an elemental condition. Again we find through this same elemental condition—water—we begin with the first forms of life. First those of the nature without body, without the elemental forces of even propagation. Again these grow into that form of able to move and begin then to multiply, by the division, forming then the first cell forces. In cell forces, then, we have taken on the first principle of the beginning of that as is seen in the evolution of an ideal in that brain force or center. Hence we find reincarnation, resuscitation, and that of the re-inhibition [re-inhabitation?], becoming a portion of those very conditions as the first principle in same, or the very first experience in same, to the body mind of [900], presented in this.

Reading 826-8

Q: Must each soul continue to be reincarnated in the earth until it reaches perfection, or are some souls lost?

A: Can God lose itself, if God be God—or is it submerged, or is it as has been given, carried into the universal soul or consciousness? The *soul* is not lost; the *individuality* of the soul that separates itself is lost. The reincarnation or the opportunities are continuous until the soul has of itself become an *entity* in its whole or has submerged itself.

Q: If a soul fails to improve itself, what becomes of it?

A: That's why the reincarnation, why it reincarnates; that it *may* have the opportunity. Can the will of man continue to defy its Maker?

Reading 956-1

Q: What will convince me of reincarnation?

A: An experience.

Reading 452–6

Q: What part of New Testament definitely teaches Reincarnation?

A: John. Six to eight. Third to fifth. Then the rest as a whole.

2

●

Insightful Past-Life Readings by Edgar Cayce

Text of Reading 342-2 M 48
(Unemployed Executive,
Protestant Background)

This psychic reading given by Edgar Cayce at his home on Arctic Crescent, Va. Beach, Va., this 29th day of May, 1933, in accordance with request made by self—Mr. [342], Active Member of the Ass'n for Research & Enlightenment, Inc.

PRESENT

Edgar Cayce; Gertrude Cayce, Conductor; Gladys Davis, Steno. Mildred Davis, L.B. Cayce and E.B. Lindsley.

READING

Born September 4, 1884, about 7:00 A.M. in Schultzville, Pa.

Time of Reading 4:15 to 5:00 P.M. Eastern Standard Time. . . . , Ill.

(Life Reading Suggestion)

EC: Yes, we have the entity and those relations with the universe, and universal forces—that are latent and manifested in the personalities of the entity now known as [342].

In entering, we find the astrological influences that are innate (or the inhibitions of the entity) and those from the appearances, or experiences through the earth, have those been somewhat opposed one to another.

Hence there would be, only from an astrological aspect, some very varying presentations; yet their influence being inhibitions—and the entity's development rather of the intuitive influences, a great deal must be considered for the information given to be of a value to the entity in the present experience.

Coming in the present experience, then, from those influences in the combination of Jupiter and Uranus, there are rather the exceptional abilities for the entity to retain in self that which may be called knowledge, or learning; or that which may be termed the ability to correlate experiences of others in such a manner as to make them valuable to self. Not that the entity would be termed one easily influenced by group or mass thought, yet the entity—being not too credulous, not too incredulous—has the ability, through its intuitive influence that may be exercised (from Uranus), to weigh or judge well as to how a matter is presented as to its value in practical application in the experience of a body.

Hence the entity may be termed, from this experience, as an individual who would be a good organizer in any field of endeavor; and, as we find, one that would make exceptional progress in the present experience in the field that is known as industrial or commercial—or cooperative—insurance; though the entity's efforts to the present have been little in this field of activity, yet this—as we find—would offer a field that would make for the opportunity for the abilities to be used that have been innately builded in the entity's inner self, with the possibilities of making for self—in the present experience—a place that may be an enviable one in this field of endeavor.

Also from Venus' influence we find the entity is one that, in the acts of everyday affairs, is considerate of others; one with a high sense of honor, of justice, of those feelings that may be experienced by others with whom the entity may have personal or group experience.

Hence the entity is one capable of making friendships easily, yet choosing from same those who may be—in the mental and material fields—of the greatest advantage; though not advantageous to the entity's activities; for, with the sense of honor, with the thought of others, the entity is not inclined to take advantage of another, whether in social, in moral, or in commercial relations one with another, and at times has been called an individual not hardboiled enough for his own good; yet if the efforts and activities—as we find—are expended in the right direction, this characteristic, this ability to express the personality, the enthusiasm that the entity is able to work itself up to on any proposition—either mental, spiritual or material (if convinced of the sincerity, the plausibility and possibilities), may be expanded upon by the entity in such a manner as to produce enthusiasm in the efforts of those with whom the entity may surround self in any endeavor.

The entity, from the *combination* of these astrological influences, is one that is a very good judge of human nature; being naturally—from Uranian, Jupiterian *and* Venus' influence—an analyst in every act; and judging from those activities the entity may gain in this experience, though he has lost—as will be seen—in many an earth experience.

From these astrological influences that affect the body in the present, we find these as both individual and personal aspects of the entity:

One that is a student in any field in which the entity finds an innate or mental interest; and these turned toward those of the mental body, as well as commercial influences.

One that remembers dates, periods and activities, through associations of those things that deal with the response individuals make to some proposition, some term or turn, some experience, in their own life.

In this also we find one that is capable of directing groups. One not so much as the leader of mob force or influence, but as an executive influence in correlating the *mental* activities of groups.

One that finds some little details that become as hobbies to the entity, in gathering about self things that to others have—and to self has—little commercial value, yet a great deal of sentiment attached to those things that the entity holds or keeps rather as hobbies in the entity's experience for diversion in the varied fields of activity.

As to the appearances, then, and their effect upon the entity in the

present experience, in drawing a comparison for an entity, here we find
a condition that may be well to give as an explanation for the entity's
own application; while it would not be always wholly applicable in the
experience of others that are balanced in an opposite manner, or a variation, from that which has been indicated for the entity:

While there are those karmic influences that must be met, because of
that which has been builded by an entity (that retains, maintains, kin-
ship with the Creative influences), it must of itself meet that which is the
measure according to the law as related to universal forces. Or, to put it
in another manner:

It is not all for an entity, or a soul, to have knowledge concerning
law; whether karmic law, spiritual law, penal law, social law, or what
not. The *condition* is, what does the entity *do about* the knowledge that is
gained! Is the knowledge used to evade cause and effect, or is it used to
coerce individuals into adhering to the thoughts of self? or is it used to
aid others in *their* understanding *of* the law, and *thus* bring the cause to
that position where the *will* of the Creative influence is supreme; or the
power that comes with making the will one *with* the law of love, of
karma, of cause and effect, of every influence—one *with* Creation!

Hence the conditions that will be seen in the experiences of the entity now known as [342] in the earth's plane:

In the one before this we find the entity was in and about that place,
or plain, known as Fort Dearborn, during those periods when there was
the establishing of the relationships with the peoples of the north country and the peoples of the eastern and southern country.

The entity then was among the peoples of the north country that
were sent as emissaries, or to deal with the situations in the trading of
that the peoples of the north country had to offer in exchange for those
things made, created or imported into the land from other countries.
Hence, not as a trader but as a mediator *for* the traders in their various
capacities did the entity, then as Pericho, gain and lose in this experience. For, seeing how there might be brought about the taking of all
that was then in possession of the post, for those peoples of the much
larger powers in numbers, the entity then urged rather that there be the
possessing of same without the formality of returning an exchange for
same of equal value, and the entity lost. Yet, with the hardships that

came about, with the losing of control over those the entity would in the experience direct, the entity learned a lesson, in bodily suffering as well as in the *condemning* of *self* for the position taken.

And each soul may find that self-condemnation becomes, after all, the hell in which it finds itself in the transition periods.

Hence in the present experience the entity finds much of the commercial field being of interest, especially that as in relationships to the trading between groups, masses and individuals; yet the field that offers an assurance and a security for individuals or groups may be made the more satisfactory to the entity in the present experience. [See 342-1 indicating he was in the Royalist Army during the American Revolution.]

In the one before this we find the entity was in that period when there were the gatherings of the peoples to enter into the holy wars.

The entity then was among the Crusaders that, with Bruce and others, started for the Holy Land.

Then the entity was a zealot for those of the few that would impel all to come under one rule of order, if not by persuasion then by coercion, and the entity gained and lost through this experience; for, entering into the lands about the Holy Land, being among those of the prisoners that were turned to those that were—to the entity in the beginning—as heathen, these became through their acts of kindness—such that the entity was rather inclined to be of a different mind, and became a zealot in *this* direction. Hence the entity was termed by many as a turncoat, or as one that rebelled for self's own interests; yet the entity gained in the latter portion, feeling and knowing—through the experience of that period—that *truly* all force, all power of a spiritual or mental nature, emanates from a *one* source.

Hence in the present there is seen that much thought is given to the spiritual side of life.

Hence in fields of activity in which the home or the associations, or the business relations, may be *assured* to peoples—for not only the material, but for the mental aptitudes and welfare *of* groups, may the entity find a channel through which it may gain the greater self- development in the present experience.

Then the entity was in the name Charleon, and was of a northern and a southern France connection in that period.

In the one before this we find the entity was in that land now known as the Persian, among those peoples that had gathered in the hill and plain country for the teachings that were being given by a leader in the city that was established there, of tents; later being among the first wood buildings in this particular portion of the land.

The entity was among those that made for the gathering of those things that were as foods or provisions for the peoples; hence entering into the trading with the peoples in the various lands, as they brought their wares from the south, from the east, from the north, from the west, for *exchange* in this particular region.

Through this experience the entity gained most, for—coming under the direct influence of those that had been raised in their activities by the leader in this period (Uhjltd)—the entity, then in the name Phar–Zar, gained; and when the breaking up came by the invasion of the Greeks from the north, the entity was among the first that fell under this raid or insurrection.

So, in the present, the entity finds those influences that are seen in sympathy; in maintaining about self those things that have not so much of the commercial value but a great deal of value from what the little things present in the experience of a body.

In the one before this we find the entity was in that land now known as the Nubian, during those periods when the priests from Egypt were exiled. The entity came under the direction of the high priest that was banished, and with the return of these peoples to their possessions—or to their own lands, in the building up of that which enabled not only the Egyptian progress, but the Arabian, Indian, Mongolian, Carpathian, and the Carthaginian mountains even—the entity was among those who aided in establishing for these various peoples those things of commercial value, as well as those posts for the ministrations to the physical needs of peoples.

Hence in the present is seen the particular interest of the entity in the reports that come from foundations, or from efforts of groups of people in all quarters of the globe. The entity has often wondered in self why such an interest in such data, when so little in common with same; and it would be—and is—one of the best proofs to the entity of these experiences in the earth's plane (or reincarnation).

Then the entity was in the name Hap-Zta.

As to the abilities of the entity, that to which it may attain in the present experience—and how:

We find, as we have indicated through those relationships builded innately—as personality and individuality of the entity, through the experiences in the earth and through the sojourns in these spheres about the earth, there are the influences builded in the entity making for the assuring of better conditions, better positions, of the peoples in the home. Though there may be the stalking of those things that make people afraid, through those material and spiritual influences that may be builded in the hearts of the young and the old, in *these* things may the entity build in the present that which will make for not only the *material* development, but the mental and soul development also.

Ready for questions.

Q: What did I come here to do?

A: To overcome all those things you've undone!

Q: Should I continue to use the initial S in my signature? [As advised by numerologist Ed Hall? formerly known as Victor George]

A: W would be better than S. If preferable (and such conditions— there are some reasons why this should be retained), we would continue to use the S. W would have been better, had it been chosen.

Q: What can I do that I can best succeed in, at the same time render the best service to humanity?

A: That pertaining to cooperative or industrial insurance.

We are through for the present.

Reading 993-4

Q: Can you now tell me what was my full name in my last reincarnation as a Fairfax?

A: Nettie F.

Q: What was the full name of my father at that time?

A: John D. Fairfax.

Q: Is there any record of this? If so, where can it be located?

A: There is a record that may be had from a *Mrs.* Fairfax (whose address may be had) in Washington; from the beginnings. It is of the Edwards family but brings is this.

Q: Please give details as to how my sister [560] then, Geraldine Fairfax, lost her life in being crushed in the earth. At what age was she?

A: Just the beginning of the teens, when there were those cave-ins from the preparations of some buildings in that period.

Q: How did it happen? Was she just playing around them?

A: Playing around; and then there were those activities from the earth trembling.

Reading 707-1

Q: About how much time have I spent in reincarnation up to the present time?

A: Almost in all the cycles that have had the incoming from period to period hast thou dwelt. Thine first incoming in the earth was during those periods of the Atlanteans that made for the divisions. Hence, counting in time, some twenty thousand years.

Reading 364-1 (A returning Atlantean)

Be it true that there *is* the fact of reincarnation, and that souls that once occupied such an environ are entering the earth's sphere and inhabiting individuals in the present, is it any wonder that—if they made such alterations in the affairs of the earth in their day, as to bring destruction upon themselves—if they are entering now, they might make many changes in the affairs of peoples and individuals in the present? Are they, then, *being* born into the world? If so, what *were* their environs—and will those environs mean in a material world today?

Text of Reading 1210-3 M 55

This Psychic Reading given by Edgar Cayce at his home on Arctic Crescent, Virginia Beach, Va., this 24th day of August, 1937, in accordance with request made by the New York Study Group #5 of the Ass'n for Research & Enlightenment, Inc.

PRESENT

Edgar Cayce; Gertrude Cayce, Conductor; Gladys Davis, Steno. Hugh Lynn Cayce.

READING

Time of Reading 3:40 to 4:00 P.M. Eastern Standard Time.

(Physical Suggestion)

GC: We, the members of the N.Y. Group of the Ass'n for Research & Enlightenment, engaged in a project to investigate reincarnation, have read and discussed the reading given us thru this channel June 29, 1937 [5753-2], advising us as individuals and as a group how we are to proceed in this work. We accept the instruction with the proper ideal as we understand it. We now ask for further guidance.

The members of the group actively seeking information are: [1058], [954], [1000], [189], [903], [255], [5416], [520], [1210], [165], [257], [1192].

We hope at this time to gain a better understanding of spiritual values through information on the lives of [1210], [759], [189], and [257] as these entities expressed themselves during the American Revolutionary period.

We first ask information concerning the activities and the remaining evidences of activities during the American Revolutionary period of the entity now known as [1210]—known at that time as McQuade or Quer and by the first name of Herman.

You will have before you the enquiring mind of the entity [1210], born Nov. 4, 1881, Niagara Falls, N.Y., and now of . . . St., N.Y.C., who seeks information on his past incarnation in the American Revolutionary period. You will answer the questions which have been submitted.

EC: (Not responding to first suggestion, had to be repeated—and then only responding to last paragraph of suggestion—"Enquiring mind of [1210], born Nov. 4, 1881—Aug. 24, 1937—'36, '35—" etc., on back to birth date.

Yes—much better were these presented from the information that has been given, and its period, or else there is to be sought the reflection of the whole of the experience as from the beginning. We will seek here. (Mumbling over name, birth date, place of birth, etc.)

Yes, we have the records of that entity now known as [1210]; this with the interpretations as we have had here before.

In considering the experience of the entity during that period of the American Revolution, we find that the entity served especially in those activities or campaigns about portions of Jersey, Pennsylvania and Maryland.

The entity then, as we have indicated, was in the name McQuade—Quer—McQuade—Herman; born then in the experience in what is now a portion of Connecticut; and the training and the activities just prior to the Revolution were in a partial medical course. Then the activities during the Revolution were in what would be called in the present the caring for the protective forces about the camps as respecting the health. The entity, to be sure, was among the forces that served under Washington; more direct under Lee [Henry Lee, American general, called "Light Horse Harry"], who was active in the campaign in that particular portion of the land; yet coming as a supervisor or superintendent of many of the various sites or camps, or especially during the distress of the armies of the colonists at the time.

Hence as has been indicated, we find arising from the experiences of the entity during that sojourn the capacities in the attempting to cast out fear. For it was experienced by the entity during that period that when there could be aroused within the minds and the hearts and the experiences of the emotional forces of the individuals the awareness that there were purposes greater or beyond the self, these brought the possibilities, the abilities, the activities that made for the sustaining influences. And much of that was imbued into the minds of those during the trying periods, when the fires of patriotism burned low during that severe winter in Valley Forge.

And these are the parts, the principles then that should be studied, if there would be knowledge gained of a nature that becomes a constructive experience in the activities of those in the present; that which is creative *grows*, that which is destructive is already deteriorating.

Thus these live as those influences *within* the innate forces of the soul's expression through experiences in the earth, and give rise to that which surrounds the activity of an individual entity.

Thus, as has been indicated, we have continually before us good, evil; life, death—a choice to be made.

And ever is the choice according to the *ideals* of the entity, as it gives expression of the forces and influences in its experience.

The entity then was among those that endured until after the periods of the Brandywine, when there were those effective activities; yet to the entity the injuries that were brought made for the ending of the physical experience of Herman McQuade—or Quer—in or during that portion of the latter part of the southern Pennsylvania or the New Jersey campaign, just before the change from Lee's rebuke and the activities in the Maryland land and the rise to the arousing through the activities of Sumter.

In the period then, as to days, as to that which may be a record: We find in the cemetery, in what is a Trenton station or near to same, H. McQuade—1779—17—No, it's nearly erased here—Herman McQuade, H. McQuade—H. McQuade—1777-9—177—seventeen seventy?

Ready for questions.

Q: Please correctly spell the name.

A: Q-u-a-d-e.

Q: Where is this name recorded in a document which we can find now?

A: In the rebuke of Lee by Washington. Library—Washington.

Q: Under what commanding officers did he serve?

A: As given.

Q: In what encampments did he serve?

A: As given.

Q: Can we find any evidences of these sites and where?

A: No evidences as we find at the sites.

Q: In what battles was he engaged?

A: Not so much in the battles save as in Brandywine when the injury came that brought dissolution.

Q: Was he an officer and of what rank?

A: Not as an officer but what would be called today as in the quartermaster division, or the superintendent of the health.

Q: Follow for us the movements of the entity with the American Revolutionary Army giving us various points or battlefields. At which, if any, of these can we find remaining evidences and what?

A: We have given these. Connecticut born; activities there; and when there was the abandoning of New York moved with the armies to then the Jersey and Pennsylvania and later a portion of the Maryland campaign; following through those periods of Valley Forge—or to the activities of Brandywine—and then the death there.

Q: Is there a record of baptism?

A: We do not find same.

Q: Where did he make his home in the Colonies?

A: In Connecticut.

Q: How and when did McQuade die?

A: From injuries received in Brandywine.

We are through for the present.

Text of Reading 5366-1 F 53
(Housewife, Protestant)

This Psychic Reading given by Edgar Cayce at the office of the
Association, Arctic Crescent, Virginia Beach, Va., this 19th
day of July, 1944, in accordance with request made by the
self—Mrs. [5366], Associate Member of the Ass'n for Research & Enlightenment, Inc.

PRESENT

Edgar Cayce; Gertrude Cayce, Conductor; Gladys Davis,
Jeanette Fitch, Stenos.

READING

Born October 31, 1890, on a farm near . . . , Ohio.

Time of Reading Set bet. 3:30 to 4:30 P.M. Eastern War Time.
. . . , Mass.

GC: You will give the relations of this entity and the universe, and
the universal forces; giving the conditions which are as personalities,
latent and exhibited in the present life; also the former appearances in
the earth plane, or giving time, place and the name, and that in each life
which built or retarded the development for the entity; giving the abilities of the present entity, that to which it may attain, and how. You will
answer the questions, as I ask them:

EC: My! Some very interesting characters have been born near
Bellefontaine! This entity was among those with that one who persecuted the church so thoroughly and fiddled while Rome burned. That's
the reason this entity in body has been disfigured by structural conditions. Yet may this entity be set apart. For through its experiences in the

earth, it has advanced from a low degree to that which may not even necessitate a reincarnation in the earth. Not that it has reached perfection but there are realms for instruction if the entity will hold to that ideal of those whom it once scoffed at because of the pleasure materially brought in associations with those who did the persecuting.

In giving the interpretation, then, of the records of this entity, there is much that may be said but, as has been indicated, we would minimize the faults, and we would magnify the virtues. Thus may little or nothing be given that would deter the entity in any manner from holding fast to that purpose which has become that to which it may hold. For, as Joshua of old, the entity has determined (and sometimes the entity becomes very disturbed) "Others may do as they may, but as for me, I will serve the living God."

Astrological aspects would be nil in the experiences of the entity. (Let's pray with the entity.) No such may be necessary in the experience again in the earth–materiality.

Remember, there are material urges and there are materials in other consciousnesses not three–dimensions alone.

As to the appearances in the earth, these would only be touched upon, as indicated, to be a helpful experience for the entity, as:

Before this we find the entity was in the land of the present nativity, through the experiences in seeking for new undertakings with the associates or companions. The entity became a helper to those who sought to know more of that which had been the prompting of individuals to seek freedom and to know that which is the spirit of creation or creative energies. Thus did the entity grow in attempting to interpret man's relationship to the Creative Forces or God. The name then was Jane Eyericson.

Before that we find the entity, as mentioned, was a companion or associate of that one [Nero] who persecuted those who believed in, those who accepted faith in righteousness, in goodness, in crucifying of body desires, in crucifying the emotions which would gratify only appetites of a body, either through the physical self or through physical appetites of gormandizing, and of material desire for the arousing more of the beast in individual souls. [See 33-1, Par. 10-A.]

In the experience, then, the entity is meeting self in that which was a part of the experience as Emersen.

Before that we find the entity was in the land when the children of promise entered into the promised land, when there were those whose companion or who father [Achan] sought for the gratifying of selfish desires in gold and garments and in things which would gratify only the eye. The entity was young in years and yet felt, as from those things which were told the entity, that a lack of material consideration was given the parent. The name then was Suthers.

Before that we find the entity was in the Egyptian land. The entity was among those who were trained in the Temple Beautiful for a service among its fellow men, contributing much to the household and the establishing of homes. Thus is the home near and dear to the entity, as are members of same, whether of the body-family or of the help or kinsmen.

Thus again may the entity find, in its application of those tenets and truths in the present, that answering in experiences of the entity in that land.

Then the entity was called Is-it-el.

As to the abilities:

Who would tell the rose how to be beautiful; who would give to the morning sun, glory; who would tell the stars how to be beautiful? Keep that faith! which has prompted thee. Many will gain much from thy patience, thy consistence, thy brotherly love.

Ready for questions.

Q: What locality is best for me?

A: In the middle west.

Q: What has been the incentive to heal and help others?

A: Read just what has been given.

Q: Should we invest a small sum of money in Tung Oil or Ramie land in the south, or a log cabin on a mountain side on . . . 's farm at . . . , Conn., for future vacations?

A: No. Those in the west we would prepare, or Ohio, Indiana, or Iowa. These would be the better and there invest; whether in Illinois, in oil, yes; Iowa, a rest home, yes; in Ohio, farmland.

Q: How have I been associated in the past with my husband, [4921]?

A: In the experience before this there were associations in which each was an incentive or a helper, and yet never closely associated. That's why ye disagree at times in the present. In the experience in Egypt in the same association as in the present, as were the children, though there were many more of them there.

Q: My son, [5249]?

A: As indicated.

Q: My son, [5242]?

A: As indicated.

Q: How can I best help them in the present?

A: In helping them to study to show themselves approved unto God, workmen not ashamed, rightly stressing the words of truth and keeping self unspotted from the world.

We are through with this reading.

Text of Reading 1020-2 F 39
(Housewife, Christian Background)

This psychic reading given by Edgar Cayce at the David E. Kahn home, 44 West 77th St., Apt. 14-W, New York City, this 18th day of October, 1935, in accordance with request made by the self—Mrs. [1020], Associate Member of the Ass'n for Research & Enlightenment, Inc.

PRESENT

Edgar Cayce; Hugh Lynn Cayce, Conductor; Gladys Davis, Steno. Mrs. [1020].

READING

Born February 17, 1896, in New Haven, Conn.

Time of Reading 11:25 to 12:00 A.M. Eastern Standard Time.
. . . , New York.

(Life Reading Suggestion)

EC: Yes, we have the entity and those relations with the universe and universal forces, that are latent and manifested in the personalities of the entity now known as [1020].

These, as we find then, are as records of the activities of the entity in its relationships to the universal influences that may manifest in, or be manifested by, the entity in the experiences in the earth and the environs about the earth that are termed as astrological aspects in an entity's experience.

Coming, as we find, under those influences in Venus, Mercury, Jupiter, Uranus, that are accredited with representing—or that have been determined by the sages of old as representing—individual activities, we find:

Mercury as the mind, Venus as love, Jupiter as the broadening—the larger opportunity, the expansion of influence and activity—these are but terms, that represent in an entity's influence a definite *innate* activity in the entity's experience.

In Venus we find that, irrespective of the entity's application of same—however, the entity is one making for friendships that are lasting in the experience.

One capable of becoming more and more necessary in the experiences of those whom the entity contacts.

One that is faithful in its relationships to that it has promised itself or others.

These are as innate and manifested in the manners in which the entity may make application of those experiences in the inner self, as it is related to others.

In Mercury we find the high mental abilities, yet experiences in same that make for the doubting in self as to its own capacities often.

Hence, in conjunction with the Venus influence, it produces a tendency within the experience for the entity to depend oftentimes upon those whom it has learned that are or whom it considers as being capable of judging experiences or activities.

This makes for that which at times becomes confusing to the entity, as to whether that which has been activative has been by its own mental abilities or influenced by others.

Hence we will find that especially in the activities as a *writer* would there become most helpful experiences, where the entity applied such activities in the earth in its relationships to construction of those things that may be made manifest in its activity as a writer. Or as one who would be a good judge of the efforts of others in these directions. If the entity would apply self, these activities would make or the stabilizing of these innate influences in the experience of the entity.

In Jupiter we find the broadening, or the tendency for the entity to become associated with influences upon rather than by others. For the influence the entity may have from others is individual, while the influence the entity may have upon others is rather more the universal—by the very indications of those experiences that have been indicated as to how the influences or activities of the entity may be used to give expression to those developments that have been in the *mental* or soul experience of the entity. It tends towards the experience that may be termed as innate, or as *feeling* those conditions rather than reasoning from what may be termed cold reason. This makes for those conditions where the entity may in its applications of its abilities become as one that may influence the affairs of others a very great deal by its expressions that may reach masses of peoples.

As to the appearances in the earth, then, and those that we find making for an influence in the present experience, we find:

Before this the entity was in that land now known as or called England, during those periods when there were great numbers of people entering the new land; not only for the religious freedom but for the opportunities and for the activities that would make for the growing into advantages to be had in the varied activities during the experience.

The entity heard about such activities, listened and was persuaded; yet not until the latter portion of the experience—or until the middle of the life during that particular period—did the entity come to, or become a part of the activities in, that land in and about what is now Hartford, in the land of present nativity.

There we find the entity then, in the name of Marge Condon, became as an active influence in the establishing of those that became the teachings, or the schools, or those things that had to do with the training of the young.

Hence we find in the present experience of the entity that the interests of the young are of a special interest to the entity; the care of those under varying conditions—these have been and are of a special interest. And the manners in which various sects, states or groups or societies form for the activities in these directions become innately and manifestedly a portion of the entity's thought. And again activity in these directions, *especially* as related to combining same in treatise, in manners in which same may be presented to others, would become a life work.

However, as indicated in the ruling influence of Venus in the *innate* forces, home and home conditions are ever in the expressions of the entity also.

Combining these, then, there may be made an activity; not so much that would separate the entity from other associations but that would make for an experience in the entity's life or experience in the present that would become more and more worth while, more and more appreciated, more and more helpful to others.

Before that we find the entity was in the Grecian experience when there were those periods of the first activities that began the influence as to the adorning of the bodies for sculpture and art, that pertained to these phases of man's experience. It was also when there were begun the interpretations of speech, of those things that may be termed in the present the dramatic experiences of song, verse, that there might be brought to others the influence that same had upon the activities of *groups*.

The entity then was among those that were active in such directions; not as a man (for men then were the greater actors in all these roles) but rather one who assisted in aiding such to become efficient and proficient in such activities. The entity made the designs for what in the present would be termed the costumes, and laid out such experiences.

In the present those experiences are manifested in the entity being a judge of such things, an interpreter—to self oft—without giving expression, owing to the fears that arose from the submerging of the entity in the experience. For the material self was submerged, as well as the mental and spiritual, which brought decreasing or distressing experiences in the activities.

In the present, though, these make for the abilities of judgments upon actors, or interpreters, or those that would become interested in such activities.

These only need fanning, as it were, into that innate within self, to become an experience that may be applied with those in the home building or in the training of those that are developing in mind and body.

The name then was Constance.

Before that we find the entity was in that now known as the Egyptian land, during those periods when there were the establishing of the tenets and the teachings of the Priest. It was when there was begun the preparation of those things pertaining to the establishing of what has grown in the present, from heights in other lands, to the medical reaction, the educational reaction in the various fields; the establishing of periods and areas where there were the gatherings of stones, the cutting of stones. And these became a portion of the entity's activity in that particular experience.

The entity was young in years from the earthly viewpoint when it began its service and activity in the Temple Beautiful, growing in its interest in the Temple Dance or the temple activity that *interpreted the emotions* of individuals in their service before the populace, as well as before those who made for the concentration or consecration of themselves for service in specific directions.

Later the entity became associated with those who prepared the garments of service in the Temple and in the service among those in high places.

And *especially* was the entity interested in those that had the settings of the stones, that were known as the emblems of the life of the individuals.

These were so impressed that in the present we find emblems, symbols, stones, carvings, become as something of an interest to the entity.

Throughout that experience, in the name Han-Shu-Put, the entity gained.

As to the abilities of the entity in the present, then, and that to which it may attain and how:

As the activities have been in those fields in which *others* became imbued with faith and hope in the very actions of the entity, so may the entity in the present *use* the abilities that have been gained not only in the material things or material expressions in the earth but as related to those things gained through the interims in which the soul growth has found, does find, expression.

In these manners may the entity find soul development, harmony in its relationships to its fellow man; increasing its confidence and faith in self as it finds its true relationships to the *inner* self and to the Creative Forces from without.

These, then, are the activities as we find in the present:

Stimulate the minds of those that seek expression in given directions of activity, as those seeking for an experience or a career in certain fields of activity as indicated. As interpreters, entertainers in some directions—the entity may counsel well with such.

Then, for giving that which is *innately* the experience of self—this may be done in writing and interpreting that which may be most helpful to others in the training of the young, and of those in the various ages or stages of their development, *for* some specific field of activity.

For, as will be the experience of the entity:

If you would have life, hope, faith, then *give* life, hope, faith, to those about you—in every way. For the law is, "As ye sow, so shall ye reap." If ye would know good, do good to others. If you would know the Father and His love to His creatures, show forth in thy life and in thy relationships to others that love. And in so doing does there come into the heart and mind and soul that awareness of His presence, that has been and is promised to all who seek to know His face.

Ready for questions.

Q: What were the relations in the past lives with my present husband, and just how can I be of the greatest help to him now?

A: Rather was the husband the critic of self in its attempts in the Grecian activity. Hence there have been and are at times in the present the periods when the entity becomes rather discouraged at those experiences that arise. Yet in patience and in counseling with the mate in those things where there is the *necessity* for the husband to stand in judgment upon the efforts of others, in their construction of those things or writings or conditions that are to influence great numbers of people, in this way and manner may those experiences not only become as things that would be "a working out," as it were, but become more helpful to him in the present relationship.

Q: What have been the relations in the past with my son, and how can I be of the greatest help to him?

A: As the son was in the closer relationships during those periods of the first establishing of the activities in this land of the present nativity, in his own experiences, so may the entity in the present lend the greatest aid and help through counsel, and patience. Not in railings, not in finding fault, but rather in the gentle guidance; not as duties only, but as opportunities—pointing out such in the experiences of the son.

Q: What were the relations in the past lives with my daughter, and how can I be of help to her?

A: Here we find rather a conflicting influence, from those experiences in the Egyptian activities of the entity. And these made for, then, the necessities for the aids to be the greater in showing dependence and confidence in much that has at times *riled* self, as to the choices made by the daughter. This should be done not through condoning, but through reasoning and counsel—in which the entity in that experience grew from the various activities. And it may be seen that it is over those very things in which the entity was the most active—in dress and relationships—that the misunderstandings have arisen and do arise at times; over those smaller things.

Patience endureth, if the entity will know even its strength and power.

Q: Are there any records available now of the entity's activities in Hartford?

A: As we find, among the older records of an *insurance* organization there may be found some of those records of those with whom the entity was very closely associated.

Q: What were the dates of the Grecian period referred to?

A: Just preceding what is termed in thy common parlance as the Christian era.

We are through for the present.

Text of Reading 5328-1 M 21
(Soldier, Overseas, Christian Background)

This Psychic Reading given by Edgar Cayce at the office of the Association, Arctic Crescent, Virginia Beach, Va., this 6th day of July, 1944, in accordance with request made by the self, Mr. [5328], new Associate Member of the Ass'n for Research & Enlightenment, Inc., recommended by Mr. Hugh Lynn Cayce and the book, *There Is a River.*

PRESENT

Edgar Cayce; Gertrude Cayce, Conductor; Gladys Davis and
Jeanette Fitch, Stenos.

READING

Born October 15, 1922, in Harrisburg, Pennsylvania.

Time of Reading Set bet. 3:30 to 4:30 P.M. Eastern War Time.

. . . , N.Y.

GC: You will give the relations of this entity and the universe, and
the universal forces; giving the conditions which are as personalities,
latent and exhibited in the present life; also the former appearances in
the earth plane, giving the development for the entity; giving the abilities of the present entity, that to which it may attain, and how. You will
answer the questions, as I ask them:

EC: Yes, we have the records here of that entity now called [5328].

In giving the interpretations of the records here, there is much to be
chosen from, but these we give with the desire and purpose that this
may be a helpful experience for the entity, enabling it to better fulfill
the purpose for which it entered this present sojourn.

As we find, there are many abilities. There are many conditions which
would be given, though, as warnings for the entity. For there are some
definite and latent urges that may tend to lead the entity into those
activities which would become burdensome, troublesome, discourag-
ing to the body.

Little or nothing that has to do with commercial field for this particular entity. Yet it would make a very good salesman, but those activities of the entity should have to do with things not of a concrete nature.
Thus we might find these as urges and interesting experiences for the
entity:

The entity would make a very good doctor or a very good nurse and
yet the practical side would become such a drudge that the entity would
surely break off into politics, and that would be the end of the individual entity, the individuality.

Those things which would pertain to writing especially those things
that would have to do with metaphysical subjects or the study of the
mind. Then, as a reporter or a writer would be the better manner for the

entity to develop or train itself, when there are those opportunities or experiences for the entity to prepare itself for its future activities.

Also the entity is very social-minded and yet should not marry until it is at least twenty-eight to twenty-nine years of age, or thirty-one or thirty-two would even be better, and then someone either born in January, June or October. These will be those activities which would come nearer in keeping with that in which the entity should, could, make the best associations.

In analyzing, and as to the manner in which we find the urges from astrological aspects: These urges are not as of that termed astrological, but rather because of a consciousness of the entity in those environs indicated in Mercury, with Uranus.

Thus we will find the entity at times becoming very extreme and loud in its praise, or in its denunciation, of certain conditions, or of individuals, or of certain types of matters or of things as in concrete activity. Laws, rules, regulations, some of these, too, will come in for the entity's praise or denunciation. These are, then, problems to be met within the entity's own experience and its study.

The entity, then, should study not only statesmanship or political economy but psychology and journalism also. These would be well, at those changes which will be brought about for the entity, in any good southern school; as Washington and Lee, Alabama or Florida.

These are, then, the comparisons needed in the entity's experience or unfoldment or development. Then if there is the choice for the writing, or for the speaking, or for activities in which there may be combinations of these, we will find the entity fitted for such conditions.

Do have the experience of being a cub reporter. Do have that experience of writing articles for Sunday supplements as well as scientific magazines.

Do study political economy of organizations, as some definite union and as to what their ideals and purposes are.

As to the activities in the earth, as we find, while all may not be indicated here, these give a pattern or as to how urges are latent and manifested:

Before this we find the entity was in the land of the present nativity during the early period of settling in the land, and thus in the eras when there were definite conditions, definite provisions, definite activities for groups under certain study; yet these were for freedom; these were for brotherhood; these were for activities which would bring a united effort; and these are latent in the experience of the entity in the present.

For the entity then was what might have been called a booster for the various groups of young peoples, in much the same manner, yet under quite different names, as would be the head of "4-H" Clubs in the present.

The entity was then in the name Lawrence Vance and quite active in organizing young peoples for definite services in definite group activities through the land. In the experience the entity gained and yet in the activity there came about little grudges of individuals, and these are the weaknesses in the present.

Don't let self get over-riled because ye become supersensitive to certain activities in either groups or in organizations, or for individual activities.

Before that we find the entity was in the English land when there were those preparations of individuals for activities in the church.

The entity was among those who were very definite in bringing certain lessons to groups, as to how to study natures of things, nature of individuals through those early periods. A monk, yes, in those activities just before there were those actions for Crusades in the land.

Thus the entity, as indicated, was at times overzealous of certain positions or subjects. These are indicated in the tenseness or the intense manner in which the entity may take hole of, or as just the opposite, a laggard entirely on certain conditions that do not appeal to the entity.

So, if the entity were ever to enter the commercial field, have somebody look after the business—you can do the selling—but have somebody else take care of the money, you would tend to spend it before you have it. These are not so well for one whose vision is too broad for a commercial experience or life.

Before that we find the entity was in the Holy Land in the periods when the Master walked in the earth. The entity was among those who were of the "seventy" who were chosen—not among the "twelve"—but acquainted with and knew of most of the activities. But with announcements or pronouncements, when there was the return, that one must eat of the body, and drink of the blood if they are to know the Lord, like many others the entity went away, but kept in touch with the activities; and with the day of Pentecost, when many were turned, the entity again became one of those associated with organized work. For then the entity understood, when there had been explained how on the night He was betrayed He took bread and broke it saying, "This is my body," and with the cup, "This is my blood."

For the Christ, as manifested in Jesus, was the first, is the foremost, is the essence of both bread and of wine. For that element which is life-giving physically of bread, or that giveth strength to wine, is the source of life itself. Thus in partaking, one does literally partake of the body and of the blood in that communion.

In these the entity was known as Joseph—not a companion of any of the Disciples—but rather from the land of the Galileans and thus of the Samaritan group. In the experience the entity gained, lost, gained.

The experience was of the interest in the healing, being able, by the blessing of the Master, to heal physically and mentally; which brought, has brought, still brings that interest in the spiritual side, yet don't ever attempt to be a preacher, ye failed then, ye would fail again. The activities must be, then, not ever as that which is called too practical; not that ye are not to be practical, but the basis, the spirit of a thing, the purpose of an ideal, rather than the purpose itself or what is done.

For ye will never walk very closely in that which is called orthodox way, not even when ye write your first editorials or stories.

Before that we find the entity was in the Egyptian land during those periods when there were those activities in the days of the rebellions. The entity was among those who served close to the young King during this period. So, as the activities were in attempting to keep acquainted with what was going on, (and thus abilities as a reporter, the abilities as a story teller), these would be parts of the entity's experience through which it passed in keeping "tab" on the various groups to report to the King.

In the name then Ardelentheoue the entity was good, for it could keep its own counsel and yet keep in touch with the various groups without causing dissentions to arise because of the presence of the entity.

As to the abilities, then, that to which it may attain and how, study closer what has been indicated. Do pattern the life and follow in those suggestions if it would find itself, its abilities, its activities and know this: wander not far away from Him, who is the way, the Cross, the light, the life. For in Him must each soul love, move and have its being, indeed.

Ready for questions.

Q: *In writing, along which particular line should I follow this?*

A: As has been indicated, the metaphysical.

Q: *What have been my associations in past lives with [. . .]?*

A: In two experiences. In the experience before this when you were quite infatuated, but because of the questions which arose between "thee and thou and they" (as there were questions of those activities), ye found a great deal of fault one in the other. Ye are attracted; let this be rather a slow growth, but ye have work to do together; whether as companions will depend upon whether she would wait for thee. Don't distract yourself by having the care of a family as ye attempt to analyze self and others through the psychology of life itself.

Q: *If she would wait, would these present urges be the basis for a marriage making possible our highest mental and spiritual development?*

A: She would wait. For ye have experiences to work out, especially before this, and ye worshiped from afar as the monk; wanted to marry and couldn't, and in those experiences in the Holy Land ye were one. She led you away and led you back.

Q: *Any other advice on marriage?*

A: As has been given, don't do this too soon.

Q: *Where and in what capacity have I been associated in past lives with the following: My mother, [. . .]?*

A: In the experience when ye were in the Holy Land. She to whom ye turned oft as one to guide and keep in the right way, but she was of a different faith, as she will be as ye develop in the present, yet remaining true throughout the experience. Ye have much in common, much that ye must interpret for yourself.

Q: *My father, [. . .]?*

A: In the experience in the English land when ye argued quite a bit together.

Q: *My friend, [. . .]?*

A: In the Egyptian land when you were very good friends and very good enemies.

Q: *[. . .]?*

A: In the experience in the Holy Land.

Q: *[. . .]?*

A: In the activities in Egypt, as well as in the Holy Land.

Q: *[3605]?*

A: In the experience in Egypt.

Q: [341]?

A: In the Holy Land and in Egypt.

Q: *Any other advice?*

A: Don't marry too soon! Do go to school again! Do make of yourself a writer!

We are through.

Text of Reading 5399-2 F 28
(Housewife, Protestant)

This Psychic Reading given by Edgar Cayce at the office of the Association, Arctic Crescent, Virginia Beach, Va., this 26th day of August, 1944, in accordance with request made by the self—Mrs. [5399], Associate Member of the Ass'n for Research and Enlightenment, Inc.

PRESENT

Edgar Cayce; Gertrude Cayce, Conductor; Gladys Davis, Jeanette Fitch, Stenos.

READING

Born May 23, 1915, in Raton, New Mexico.

Time of Reading Set bet. 10:30 to 11:30 A.M. Eastern War Time. . . . , Utah.

GC: You will give the relations of this entity and the universe, and the universal forces; giving the conditions which are as personalities, latent and exhibited in the present life; also the former appearances in the earth plane, giving time, place and the name, and that in each life

which built or retarded the development for the entity; giving the abilities of the present entity, that to which it may attain, and how. You will answer the questions, as I ask them.
EC: Yes, we have the record here of the entity now known as or called: [5399].

In giving an interpretation of the relationships of this entity with the universe and universal forces, much is to be taken into consideration if those suggestions indicated would be applicable in the experience of this entity. In analyzing same from the urges which arise from the astrological as well as earthly sojourn, we find these apparent:

The entity is very easily persuaded by others. Thus, the first admonition would be: know in yourself what ye believe. Do have an ideal, spiritually, mentally, materially. Do consider what manner of individual the entity should be as in relationship to the wedded life—as to the home—as to relationships with others. The *ideal*—not just ideas. The ideals must be drawn from the spiritual concept, and remember, the mind or the mental application is the builder.

There are those tendencies for the dramatic, and thus stage, or the like, appeals to the entity. This is not an adverse influence, but must be applied in the light of ideals as to be a constructive experience, rather than just feeding the ego of the individual. Thus, the entity will make a very good director, as in any social welfare work, or as a part of a program for social service for underprivileged children, or as on a school board, where all forms of activity which are to be constructive in the life of unfolding or developing bodies and minds are to be considered. These, then, are such as should be the choice that the entity would make as to the use of its abilities.

Astrologically, we find Mercury, Jupiter, Venus as the urges, and thus the dramatical; thus the beneficial influences are as the nature of the entity.

Jupiter and Venus indicate the egotism, the beauty, music, people, things and association as being parts of the consciousness, and thus, as we find, as indicated, first *do* find thine own self, its relationship to Creative Forces, or God, and the ideal manner in which this is to be acted upon in the experience, by prayer, by meditation, knowing the variations in same, analyzing self and knowing the variation between the personality of self and the individuality of self. One will find through such analyses the manner in which the abilities which are apparent and manifest in this entity may be applied in a constructive way and manner.

As to the appearances in the earth, while all may not be indicated, these indicate the pattern through which that which appears in the present has become a part of the conscious and unconscious self in the present activity.

As in the appearance before this, we find the entity among those who were of those groups in those experience when there were the ideas of gold rush in the West. The entity was among those who, with others, started toward same.

Thus, there will be a change of scenes, a looking for ideals that will enhance the material welfare. Thus, it will be very well for the entity never to undertake games of chance, yet investments that are well thought out, in analyzing of same by self, may be means of the entity, in years to come, having material gains in the earth. Investments, then, not of that as of questionable nature.

In the activity, the entity gained—the entity lost—and from there rises the warnings.

The name then was Stella Smythe.

Before that we find the entity was in the activities in the land now known as the French land, during those periods when there were the activities for an idea—for an ideal—or in those periods when wars were made because of the possession of the holy Land by individuals who proclaimed another as a prophet. The entity, then, in the opposite sex, was one of those who made hardships for those of its own household by the activities as to prevent conditions which were questioned by the entity in relationships to others. Thus the conditions which make for questioning the self rather than the universal consciousness, and the warnings, as has been indicated.

In the Name Rene Marselle, the entity gained by the hard way. Thus, the admonition to first find self, and self's relationship to Creative Forces, or God. And *do something* about same!

Before that we find the entity was in the Holy Land during those periods when there were the journeyings from the Egyptian land to the

Promised land. The entity, then, was among those who were of the household of the children of Levi, and thus the entity was a mother to one of those who became as a Priest to those peoples. This brings into the consciousness of the entity a form of ideas and ideals that are too oft set by ritual rather than the spirit of the purpose. Yet, under those influences, as indicated, if the ideas are chosen, greater strength may be part of the experience in this sojourn.

The name, then, was Jalebd.

Before that we find the entity was in the Egyptian Land where there were those preparations of individuals for activities through the Temple of Sacrifice, as well as the Temple Beautiful, for the propagation or for the changing of activities of individuals born into the earth through the tempering of individuals' activities in the Temple of Sacrifice and the training in the Temple Beautiful.

The entity was among those who were chosen for the establishing of a home, with the departure of the Priest, in those experiences when such activities came about.

The name then was Is-tabel.

As to the abilities, these have been indicated. As to the manner of application, first, find self. Do know the ideal. Do apply same mentally, yes, but know the ideal spiritual, for from the spiritual purposes must rise that which may be manifested in the material experience of the individual.

Ready for questions.

Q: Should I try to accomplish anything in art?

A: In the art of drawing others, more than that as of higher art, yes.

Q: Have I ever caught glimpses of past lives, or are these things more dreams and fancy?

A: The entity has caught glimpses of past lives when it has gone out of itself or has allowed the energies of the kundaline force to pass along the centers of the body. Beware, unless ye are well-balanced in purposes, for there is one way. Those who climb up some other way—remember what the Master gave.

Q: How have I been associated in the past with my husband, [. . .]?

A: In the experience in the Holy Land the entity who is the husband now was a Priest of Israel in his activities.

Q: Am I justified in feeling that we shouldn't live in the same town with my husband's mother?

A: These should never be the attempt of justification, save by faith. Is the justifying being kept in accord with that which has been given as the "fruit of the spirit"? Is it being kind? Because of those conditions which arose, do to others as ye would be done by, for the Law of the Lord is perfect. It converteth the soul.

We are through with this reading.

Text of Reading 1938-2 F 78

This psychic reading given by Edgar Cayce at his home on Arctic Crescent, Virginia Beach, Va., this 29th day of June, 1939, in accordance with request made by the self—Mrs. [1938], Associate Member of the Ass'n for Research & Enlightenment, Inc.

PRESENT

Edgar Cayce; Gertrude Cayce, Conductor; Gladys Davis, Steno.

READING

Born June 7, 1861, in Brooklyn, N.Y.

Time of Reading 3:30 to 4:15 P.M. Eastern Standard Time
. . . . , N.Y.

GC: You will give the relation of this entity and the universe, and the universal forces; giving the conditions which are as personalities, latent and exhibited in the present life; also the former appearances in the earth plane, giving time, place and the name, and that in each life which built or retarded the development for the entity; giving the abilities of the present entity and that to which it may attain, and how. You will answer the questions she has submitted, as I ask them:

EC: (In going back over years from present—"—'36—'35—'34—years of anxiety—'33—'30—satisfaction—'29—'23—different periods—'22—'84—yes, unusual year—'83—" etc., on back to birth date.)

Yes, we have the records here (far spent) of that entity now known as or called [1938].

In giving the interpretations of these records—these are being chosen with the desire that the experience may be a helpful one in every way.

There may be those considerations of the virtues, the vices; that, applying the rules and regulations as should be the part of everyone's experience, there may come to the entity an appreciation and a realization of the purposes for which each soul enters a material experience.

God hath not willed that any soul should perish; hence He has given and does constantly give the opportunity for each soul's manifestation through the material plane, that there may come the greater activities in the affairs of each soul or entity to become more aware, and to apply self in that which is the justification by faith through the manner that has been shown for each individual for his or her own consideration, as to what will or will not be done respecting same.

Hence we find, as for the experiences of this entity in the material sojourn as well as the sojourn without the material plane—the urges remain as latent activities to be applied in such a way and manner as to be a light or guide unto the many in thy dealings with thy fellow man.

In the astrological aspects for this entity we find a great deal of misconception in the minds of many, yet to the entity these may be comprehended if there is the application of self in those manners in which the seeking of the soul may come to know and search for that which is the creative influence in the experiences from day to day.

The urges latent, but without respect to what the application has been or may be, are and may be a great part of that through which the entity may gain, and find in the gaining greater contentment, a greater channel for activity.

Music and musical talents are a natural part of the entity; the ability for the appreciation of same, and especially that of the pastoral nature—yet that deals with or tells its own story in the very air of same.

In the effect of the planetary forces we find Venus, Jupiter, Mercury, Saturn as the ruling forces. Hence the musical influence, as well as the love and the love of companionship, love of associations with others that have or manifest a helpful air; as well as those abilities within self to experience the variations as indicated through the Jupiterian forces of the working force about or of many individuals.

Thus we find also changes that have and do become a part of the experience.

"Seek and ye shall find" may be said to many, and yet much more to this entity than to the many. For the appearances as well as the urges from the astrological sojourn bear the relationships one to another as do the dimes to the monetary unit or dollars.

Not that the entity is inclined to become jealous of those because of their association or position, yet there is a constant searching within self for those influences that will bring all of those activities that have been indicated to the consciousness of the entity.

These while having failed often, we find that they will become more and more a part of the entity in its daily experience.

As to the appearances of the entity in the earth's plane—these are not all given, but these that have a particular influence in the present because of their influence being oft seen by the indomitable will of the entity to succeed in whatever it undertakes; not by might nor by power but by every word that proceedeth—should be as a part of that which is held constantly before self.

The appearances indicate much of those variations that have been a part of the experience, as well as the variation of abilities in which the entity may accomplish or carry forward in such a manner as not to become stalemated or in such a position that the appearances—at least—are not so variegated to the ideas or manners of others.

Before this, then, we find the entity was in the land of the present nativity, during those periods when there was the reconstruction from the activities of what is called at times the American Revolution, or American rebellion.

Yet we find the entity was among those of that period in which there were the considerations of accomplishments and activities of individuals that would enable or fit them for a social as well as an economic service within the experiences of those about the entity.

There again we find the entity was much in that position of an understanding pertaining to the study and application of a musical nature or trend.

Then in the name Marguerite Street, the entity gained, the entity lost. The entity gained in application in which there was the use of those means for raising the hopes, the desires and purposes to the beautiful associations and surroundings and environs—not only for self but making same aware in the experiences of others. When those were turned into those channels for self-indulgence or self-aggrandizement, they were brought not only disturbing forces eventually but the necessity of meeting self in those activities in its associations with others in the present.

Before that we find the entity was in the land now known as the Promised land, during those periods when there was much expectancy, much preparation on the part of those who were looking forward to the redeeming of the peoples from not only the bondage of the Roman rule but the misconception and misapplication of the laws of individuals or peoples who professed to be in the way of the chosen people.

The entity was among those who were the musicians in the temple where Anna and Simeon saw the consecration of the one Lord, the one Master.

Then the entity was a harpist, or what would be called a harp today.

Hence all manner of stringed instruments are of interest, and especially that character or nature of music that depicts the activities of individuals through those various periods in that particular activity—or that as may be a part of the experience of individuals in the present; not only that which is of the pictorial and pastoral nature but descriptive in its nature.

And to encourage, and to bring into the consciousness of the young, and those of all ages whom the entity may meet and with whom the entity may have an influence, an appreciation of such—is the greater service in which the entity may expend itself.

For this is the manner—*music*—in which distances may be spanned, in which all realms of thought may find a greater outlet of expression, and in which the heart may be raised to a comprehension of the relationships. For, as is oft expressed, the angels seeing [sing]—and the music of the spheres, as in color and relationship—this becomes the means or manner that is universal in its activity upon the minds and souls of men.

The name then was Sathamantha. In the experience the entity gained throughout.

Hence in the present periods the greater need for manifesting and expressing that as may bring the greater influence for good in the experience of this entity.

Before that we find the entity was in the land now known as the Mongoloid land, during those periods of activities when there were the attempts of the many nations, or peoples of many lands, to correlate the influences that prompted greater brotherly relationships in the experience of man—or that as may be said to be the paralleling of the experience in Egypt, in India, in Carpathia, in parts of On and Og, or the periods in the Himalayas, the Yucatan, the Andes and the Pyrenees. For there were the periods then when there was the attempt for *peace* to be wrought in the experience of man.

The entity was in the City of Gold, and among those who were high in the affairs and activities of the sun worshipers of gold—a princess, and thus making for influences in which there was the establishing of what was to be the manner of conduct of peoples of certain rank or station.

Hence we find the innate forces in which there is the love of the family tree, the relationships of the genealogy of groups or individuals, innate within the experience.

This is well—but remember, God looketh not on the outward appearance but rather upon the heart and the purpose and desire of each soul.

And He hath not willed that any should perish, but has set that manner of overcoming within thine own hands—if ye do good it is well; if ye do evil, sin lieth at thy door—or if ye think more highly of thyself than ye ought to think.

The experience brought disturbance—for such activities were in opposition to many of those tenets of the peoples from Atlantis as well as Egypt and the East Indian land—for those were impelling forces that brought the periods of the first disintegration in that land.

The name then was Ms-Sma.

As to the abilities of the entity in the present, and that to which it may attain, and how:

As indicated, in those fields or activities in the present in which encouragement may be given to those who would make song or verse, and in the giving of counsel and the impelling influences for the magnifying of the rhythm, of the nature that is pictorial yet descriptive of the various forces and emotions of men—these are the activities and channels for service.

Study then to show thyself approved unto thy Maker, a workman not ashamed, but keeping thyself in such a way and manner that thy conscience is kept aware of the union of purpose with Him whom ye sought in the Palestine hills.

Ready for questions.

Q: *In what capacity did I serve in former lives to develop an intense interest in scientific investigation and work?*

A: As indicated, in those periods when so many of the peoples and activities of the land sought to know through whom, where and whence would come the spiritual forces as were manifest in Bethlehem of Judea.

Q: *In what manner did I meet my present husband, [. . .], in past lives, and in what capacity was he serving?*

A: In the experience before this, the association was close—as one of the same family.

Through the activities in the Mongoloid land, there were rather the friendships and the forming of social relationships and activities.

Q: *Are any of my children or my grandchildren, children of former experiences?*

A: These may be best indicated by the paralleling of their own experiences through the sojourns in the earth.

Q: *Was my Palestine experience in the land of the Nativity*
at the time of Jesus the Christ?

A: Just as indicated—and the entity was at the period when the consecration of the child was made—viewed same, and later understood much with the Holy Women.

Q: *Have I progressed much in my present lifetime?*

A: Who is to say, or to be the judge? Only as has been indicated, let not thine own conscience smite thee. And keep that awareness of the closer walk with Him.

Q: *In what way, in former lives, did I contact [1152]?*

A: In the Palestine experience.

Q: *What activities should I emphasize during my present experience?*

A: As indicated, the aid and help through encouraging in every manner the form and character of information as given—or the *music* of the nature indicated.

We are through for the present.

Editor's Note: The following reading was for Edgar Cayce himself. It contains many, but not all, of his soul's past lives.

Text of Reading 294-8 M 46
(Clairvoyant, formerly a Photographer, Protestant)

This psychic reading given by Edgar Cayce at Phillips Hotel, Room 115, Dayton, Ohio, in a series of five readings beginning February 9th, 1924, one on 2/12/24, two on 2/13/24, and one on 2/16/24. Request made by Edgar Cayce himself.

P R E S E N T

Edgar Cayce; Linden Shroyer, Conductor; Gladys Davis, Steno.

R E A D I N G

Born March 18, 1877, in Christian Co., Ky., near Hopkinsville. [1:30 P.M. Central Standard Time (?).]

Time of Reading 11:40 A.M. 2411-1/2 E. 5th St., Dayton, Ohio.

(Horoscope Suggestion, with request for past lives, etc.)

EC: There is much we have given relative to this before. We have the conditions as have been, as are, and will be. In this, without reference to that as has been given, for in giving the conditions in the various phases of the past experience there will be much that will show the various phases of the developing in the different stages, the conditions as given then will be those as with reference to the effect that the planets and their satellites and spheres have upon the present life and plane, without reference to the will.

Then, with the will, and also the developing with will and the planetary or astrological effect in the various planes as have gone before; in the present, as in this plane, we find the condition as brought to the earth plane was from that of the attitudes as held by those to and through whom the present entity was and is made manifest upon the earth plane by the relativity of force and the attraction of likes; the attitude of those earthly parents towards conditions that brought the relations to the stage of the developing of the entity that came, and through that stage the entity chose the mode of manifesting in the earth plane. Hence the condition of the parents upon the earth plane, or duty that is due each of its earthly offsprings, for all are under that bond of duty to be made the channel of the manifesting of this force through the entity's actions towards his offsprings.

As to the condition from the astrological standpoint, we find this entity almost entirely influenced by, and came from that in the last plane of Uranus, with Neptune, Venus and Jupiter. Afflictions in Mars and of the Sagittarius, Capricornus, Gemini Sun and Moon in the various stages, for with the ultra forces, as of Uranus and Neptune, come much of the influence of the various planes, given in strength with Jupiter and Mercury.

As to the influences this gives then without reference to the will:

One that will always be either very good or very bad, very wicked or very much given to good works. Ultra in all forces. Very poor, very rich. One scaling to the heights in intellectual ability and capacity, or groveling in the dregs of self-condemnation, influenced at such times by those forces either coming as afflictions from the various phases of developing, from which the entity has received its experience, or controlled by will as exercised in the present sphere.

One ever within the scope or sphere of firearms, yet just without.

One saved spiritually, mentally and financially often through a great amount of waters, for it was from the beginning, and will be so unto the end of time, as time is reckoned from the earth plane, for this entity we find was first manifest in the earth plane through the waters as was on the earth, and above the earth. Hence through these elements and forces is the spiritual, mental and financial, these three phases of spiritual life, mental life and financial life manifest in the earth plane.

One who finds much in the scope or sphere of intrigue in secret love affairs. One given often to the conditions that have to do with the affairs of the heart, and of those relations that have to do with sex.

One that finds the greater strength in spiritual forces and developing.

One given to make manifest in the present plane much of the forces of psychic and occult forces, reaching the greater height of developing in such plane in those forces when that of Jupiter, with Uranus and Neptune, come within the scope of the Sun's influence upon the earth plane and forces.

One that will bring, through such manifestations, joy, peace and quiet to the masses and multitudes through individual efforts.

One who, after the present year passes that place of that of Pisces and Sun's rays on the twentieth of present month, will go forward to developing much of the psychic and occult forces to the great numbers that have become interested in developing of such phenomena.

One who will on the nineteenth of March, this year, reach the place or plane where the present years and the present developing reaches the turn for the developing, or the wield of those influences in Sagittarius, Capricornus and Gemini that may bring destructive forces without will's manifestation upon that day.

In the developing as regards will force in the present plane, with conditions, there have been many conditions that have been hindered by the effect of the will, and others that have been assisted. Keep the will in that of the spiritual development, if the physical would manifest to the better advantage in the present plane, keeping this ever before, that all work in present plane will be judged to that individual and the classes, masses, as to the individual's manifestation of spiritual forces in and through the individual action in and before men. Ever keeping the mind clear to the developing of the Uranian forces that often manifest in the present plane, which will in the present plane reach in the present and coming two years the influence of the Neptune and Mercury forces, carry the body, unless will is exercised against such conditions, to many places beyond this present bounds, or across many waters. Keep the developing then to that force as is given in that of Uranus, Neptune and Jupiter, whose greater influence as is upon the earth plane, and beware of the influences in Venus forces, for with Mars' affliction would bring sudden destruction to the physical in the early fall of present year.

As to the vocation, this in the present plane may be directed in any channel through will. The better condition, as given, in that of astrological forces, would be toward those of psychic and occult, or teaching or developing along the lines of such plane to give the manifestation of such forces to the populace.

In the plane as of others:

In the one just before this, we find in the present place of the physical plane sojourn, but in that of the soldier in the British forces as were in the force that developed in the surrounding plains. The name, John Bainbridge, and in that life we find the birth in Cornwall, England, and the training in the Canadian forces as taken by that country, and the drifting into the present plain as known as American, or United America, and the life was lost then in the waters as in the crossing of the river at the time the battle was fought near the present sojourn. In this, as that given just previous to the present appearance upon this plane, in which the body's sojourn was near unto that at present, we find the body's or the entity's and body's condition is then entered upon that of the Saturn forces, [See 5755-1 on 6/27/38] and the life was manifested then in the plane was as that of the adventurer, when the forces of the king, under whose rule this entity was a subject, entered in that force, or in the colonization of the country, was the first appearance upon this present sphere's plane or scope, and was connected with that in the group that were landing in the East coast of the new country, now known as Virginia, and near where is now the resort known as Virginia Beach. When this raid was made, this John Bainbridge was carried in this raid to the Southern coasts of the country; escaped, and with the forces then going in the inland way, and making the surrounding of the places in which the present sphere's plane has seen much of the same country, and developing, and finally making the way to the fort then on the Great Lakes, now in place known as Chicago, and from that fort entered the fray in which the crossing was later attempted in the Ohio River, and there met death as known in the earth plane. [See 294-8] The body was known as under two names, and was never wed during that sojourn upon the plane, though was in many escapades that have to do with those of the nature of the relations with the opposite sex. In the developing upon the present plane, we have much of the personality as shown in present spheres, as from that of the ability to take cognizance of detail, especially in following instructions as given from other minds or sources of information.

In that previous to this, we find in the Courts of the French, when

Louis the 15th was King, and in the Royal Guard was this entity's sphere, which was of short duration, so far as years go upon the earth plane. This entity, then, was the attendant upon the Royal Court and the Guard for the household of that Ruler, and lost the elements of life, as known, in the defense of those under whose care they were placed, as both lost the elements of physical life, in the defense. In the forces or personal conditions as seen in present sphere from this sojourn, we find that of the intense defense of those principles that to the entity's inmost soul or force is the right. In the name, we find that of Ralph Dahl [Dale?]. [In reading 1001-7, Cayce indicates that Louis the 15th and Edgar Cayce had the same grandfather; or was Louis 15th grandfather of John Bainbridge, one of Cayce's incarnations?]

In the condition that was previous to this, we find in the force as manifest when the Trojan rule was in that fair country, to whom the nations of the world have looked for the beauty in culture, art and refinement of the physical, mental and material force, and in that we find again the soldier and the defender of the gate, as was the place where the physical or material destruction came to the body. In the experience of that plane, we find these cover many and various stages. Those of the student, chemist, the sculptor and the artisan, as well as of the soldier and defender in the last days. In that we find the name Xenon, and there is, and has been, and will be many more in the present sphere that were in contact with that plane's forces, that the contact will be, has been brought in the present sphere. In this, we find those present forces exhibited through that of the art, and the love of the beautiful in any and every form, especially those that partake of human form Divine.

In that before this we have that plane in which is now known as the Arabian plane. In this we find this entity's developing under that of Uhjltd, and there are many of the conditions, personality, knowledge, understanding, thought, reference as is and will be in the passing of the plane of today. For we find there are many upon this earth's plane, and in different locations, who were associated with this entity at that time. [Persia is now known as Iran.] In the entity's force of that day, we find this entity one of power, prestige, royalty, and the leader in many raids or wars as made upon the surrounding peoples, tribes or nations. This we find the most outstanding of that period, in the connection as was shown in the war as made on the Persian ruler, Croesus, and this Uhjltd led the expedition into that country. The force under this leadership was successful in the bringing submission to the rule of the nation which Uhjltd led. And the developing in that plane was with the suffering of bodily ills from injuries received in the escape from the force as connived from the weaknesses of the physical to make the Uhjltd a slave in bondage. His escape and sojourn upon the plain, with those surrounding him, was the developing stage, and the first of that developing known in present earth plane as psychic force. For, with the developing as received in the plane just before this [in prehistory Egypt as the priest Ra Ta], as we shall see, [this Uhjltd sojourn] was the continuation of the one found at that time.

The passing of the portion of the entity again into Nazova [?] [nirvana?] was through the wounds and infections as received upon the plane, in the vicinity of the well about which the three palm trees [stood, which] has remained in the inner being of the soul's developing force. And not until that entity [538?] is again reunited with this entity [294] will the developing upon this or other planes be efficient, or as good as should be.

In the elements as brought to the present plane, we find that of the deep love as manifests to others in any or all positions or stage of conditions in life. The inert [innate] and the hidden love for animal and live creatures of the Creator's make, as was developed in this sojourn upon the plain. With the meeting or contact of this entity's mate, for upon the 19th day of March, in present year, that entity will again be in physical touch with the entity's present development, again will come the power of monies, both in the way of earth's fame and glory, and with this will again the opportunity to develop as has been set in this plane of development, and again give the place in the world development towards the mark of the higher calling, as is set in Him. Upon that meeting will the developing depend, or begin, to be made manifest, or be cut short, as the will of the entity expresses and manifests itself. In this sphere or plane, we find there are many that come under the influence of the personal or personality of the entity's forces, and for many, many years after this return to the other spheres was this influence felt in the earth's plane, as in this influence felt in the earth's plane, as in this present plane, this with this union of forces may and will give that incentive to others to develop in that plane that leads to the understanding of the forces that give of the strength of the universal force.

In the plane before this, we find that as known in the dynasty of the Rameses or Pharaohs in Egypt, and in the Court and rule of the Second Pharaoh [341] or Rameses, [10,500 B.C.] and was at that time the high priest of the cult as gave the religious element and force in the age, and reached the heights in that dynasty, yet was cut short in the allowing of physical forces and desires to enter in, and the taking of the daughter [538] of the order of the one who offered the sacrifices for the priest's force, and going or leaving the shores of this country brought the destructive elements to the body. That same entity that was taken is at present in this earth's plane, the companion and mate as should be in the present sphere [538], and in this Court we find there was the study of the religious cults, isms, schisms as would be termed in this day and plane. The High Priest [294] who gave the elements of the religious force, and in this dynasty or reign of this Pharaoh [341] did the religious cult reach its height, as given through this priest, though he became the outcast, but for the good as had been accomplished by this individual was in the resting place of the King, and the forces as manifest in the present is the delving into the whys and wherefores of all who express a different mode of manifesting the hope that lies within the human breast of the life after the passing from the earth's plane. This, we see, manifests in the present. As to those forces that have brought this condition that the entity is in, the elements as brought the destructive force to self in the two, again we find that the karma of each must be met, [294] and [538] and in this plane overcome if each would enter in.

In that before this, we find in the beginning, when the first of the elements were given, and the forces set in motion that brought about the sphere as we find called earth plane, and when the morning stars sang together, and the whispering winds brought the news of the coming of man's indwelling, of the spirit of the Creator, became the living soul. This entity came into being with this multitude. As to the experiences as have been given in this plane, the earth, and the often sojourn upon this plane, we find all summed in this:

Take this thou hast in hand and make and mould it into the present plane's development, that thyself and others may know that God is God, and demands of His creatures that of the knowledge of self, that they may better serve their fellows, and in so doing present themselves as the ever giving force, bringing to others to the knowledge of Him.

There are many other influences as have been shed abroad in the earth's plane from the entity's sojourn there. These are given that all may know and understand that the record of each soul is kept in and unto that Great Day.

Be not deceived. Be not overcome, but overcome evil with good.

3

●

Planetary Sojourns:
The Soul's Life Between Incarnations

Editor's Note: Some of the most fascinating concepts to come through Edgar Cayce's discourses were his teachings about soul activity between earth incarnations and how these affect our present lives. Here are some of these discourses.

Text of Reading 5755-1

This psychic reading given by Edgar Cayce at his office of the Association for Research and Enlightenment, Inc., Virginia Beach, Va., at the Seventh Annual Congress of the A.R.E., this 27th day of June, 1938, in pursuant to request made by those present.

PRESENT

Edgar Cayce; Gertrude Cayce, Conductor; Gladys Davis, Steno. Hugh Lynn Cayce, Gladys & Chas. Dillman from Youngstown, O., Maud M. Lewis from Greenville, Ala., Anna E. Hendley & Edna B. Harrell from D.C., Lillian McLaughlin, Gladys & Thos. Jenkins, Reginia Dunn, Florence Evylinn Campbell, Mary A. Miller, Alice M. Eddy, Irene Harrison, Louise Chisholm, Henry Hardwicke, Jennie Moore and Leslie Savage from N.Y., Mabel M. Applewhite from Newport News,

Va., Frances Y. Morrow, Edith & Florence Edmonds, Hannah
Miller, Ruth LeNoir, Helen Ellington, Margaret Wilkins, Esther
Wynne, Abbie Kemp & Malcolm H. Allen from Norfolk, Va. &
Helen Williams, Louise Tatum, Mara Edmonstone, Mrs. R. G.
Barr, Mrs. W. T. Sawyer, Grace & Geo. Ross from Virginia
Beach.

READING

Time of Reading 3:35 to 4:20 P.M.

GC: In all Life Readings given through this channel there are references to sojourns of the soul-entity between incarnations on the earth
plane, in various planes of consciousness represented by the other planets in our solar system. You will give at this time a discourse which will
explain what takes place in soul development in each of these states of
consciousness in their order relative to the evolution of the soul; explaining what laws govern this movement from plane to plane, their
influence on life in this earth plane and what if any relationship these
planes have to astrology. Questions.

EC: Yes, we have the information and sources from which same may
be obtained as to individual experiences, sojourns and their influence.

As we find, in attempting to give a coherent explanation of that as
may be sought, or as may be made applicable in the experience of
individuals who seek to apply such information, it is well that an individual soul-entity, the record of whose astrological and earthly sojourns
you have, be used as an example.

Then a comparison may be drawn for those who would judge same
from the astrological aspects, as well as from the astrological or planetary sojourns of such individuals.

What better example may be used, then, than this entity with whom
you are dealing [EC? Case 294]

Rather than the aspects of the material sojourn, then, we would give
them from the astrological:

From an astrological aspect, then, the greater influence at the entrance of this entity that ye call Cayce was from Uranus. Here we find

the extremes. The sojourn in Uranus was arrived at from what type of experience or activity of the entity? As Bainbridge, the entity in the material sojourn was a wastrel, one who considered only self; having to know the extremes in the own experience as well as others. Hence the entity was drawn to that environ. Or, how did the Master put it? "As the tree falls, so does it lie." [Eccl. 11:3 by Solomon. Where did Jesus say it?] Then in the Uranian sojourn there are the influences from the astrological aspects of *extremes*; and counted in thy own days from the very position of that attunement, that tone, that color. For it is not strange that music, color, vibration are all a part of the planets, just as the planets are a part—and a pattern—of the whole universe. Hence to that attunement which it had merited, which it had meted in itself, was the entity drawn for the experience. What form, what shape?

The birth of the entity into Uranus was not from the earth into Uranus, but from those stages of consciousness through which each entity or soul passes. It passes into oblivion as it were, save for its consciousness that there is a way, there is a light, there is an understanding, there have been failures and there are needs for help. Then help *consciously* is sought!

Hence the entity passes along those stages that some have seen as planes, some have seen as steps, some have seen as cycles, and some have experienced as places.

How far? How far is tomorrow to any soul? How far is yesterday from thy consciousness?

You are *in* same (that is, all time as one time), yet become gradually aware of it; passing through, then, as it were, God's record or book of consciousness or of remembrance; for meeting, being measured out as it were to that to which thou hast attained.

Who hath sought? Who hath understood?

Only they that seek shall find!

Then, born in what body? That as befits that plane of consciousness; the *extremes*, as ye would term same.

As to what body—what has thou abused? What hast thou used? What hast thou applied? What has thou neglected in thy extremes, thy extremities?

These are consciousnesses, these are bodies.

To give them form or shape—you have no word, you have no form in a three-dimensional world or plane of consciousness to give it to one in the seventh—have you?

Hence that's the form—we might say—"Have You?"

What is the form of this in thy consciousness? It rather indicates that everyone is questioned, "Have you?—Have You?"

That might be called the form. It is that which is thy concept of that being asked thyself—not that ye have formed of another.

With that sojourn then the entity finds need for, as it were, the giving expression of same again (the answering of "Have You?") in that sphere of consciousness in which there is a way in and through which one may become aware of the experience, the expression and the manifesting of same in a three-dimensional plane.

Hence the entity was born into the earth under what signs? Pisces, ye say. Yet astrologically from the records, these are some two signs off in thy reckoning.

Then from what is the influence drawn? Not merely because Pisces is accredited with an influence of such a nature, but because it is! And the "Have You" becomes then "There Is" or "I Am" in materiality or flesh, or material forces—even as He who has passed this way!

The entity as Bainbridge was born in the English land under the *sign*, as ye would term, of Scorpio; or from Venus as the second influence.

We find that the activity of the same entity in the earthly experience before that, in a French sojourn, followed the entrance into Venus.

What was the life there? How the application?

A child of love! A child of love—the most hopeful of all experiences of any that may come into a material existence; and to some in the earth that most dreaded, that most feared!

(These side remarks become more overburdening than what you are trying to obtain! but you've opened a big subject, haven't you?)

In Venus the body-form is near to that in the three dimensional plane. For it is what may be said to be rather *all*-inclusive! For it is that ye would call love—which, to be sure, may be licentious, selfish; which also may be so large, so inclusive as to take on the less of self and more of the ideal, more of that which is *giving*.

What is love? Then what is Venus? It is beauty, love, hope, charity—

yet all of these have their extremes. But these extremes are not in the expressive nature or manner as may be found in that tone or attunement of Uranus; for they (in Venus) are more in the order that they blend as one with another.

So the entity passed through that experience, and on entering into materiality abused same; as the wastrel who sought those expressions of same in the loveliness for self alone, without giving—giving of self in return for same.

Hence we find the influences wielded in the sojourn of the entity from the astrological aspects or emotions of the mental nature are the ruling, yet must be governed by a standard.

And when self is the standard, it becomes very distorted in materiality.

Before that we find the influence was drawn for a universality of activity from Jupiter; in those experiences of the entity's sojourn or activity as the minister or teacher in Lucius. For the entity gave for the gospel's sake, a love, an activity and a hope through things that had become as of a universal nature.

Yet coming into the Roman influence from the earthly sojourn in Troy, we find that the entity through the Jupiterian environment was trained—as we understand—by being tempered to give self from the very universality, the very bigness of those activities in Jupiter.

For the sojourn in Troy was as the soldier, the carrying out of the order given, with a claim for activities pertaining to world affairs—a spreading.

What form, ye ask, did he take? That which may be described as in the circle with the dot, in which there is the turning within ever if ye will know the answer to thy problems; no matter in what stage of thy consciousness ye may be. For "Lo, I meet thee *within* thy holy temple," is the promise.

And the pattern is ever, "have you?" In other words, have you love? or the circle within, and not for self? but that He that giveth power, that meeteth within, many be magnified?

Have you rather abased self that the glory may be magnified that thou didst have with Him before the worlds were, before a division of consciousness came?

These become as it were a part of thy experiences, then, through the astrological sojourns or environs from which all take their turn, their attunement.

And we find that the experience of the entity before that, as Uhjltd, was from even without the sphere of thine own orb; for the entity came from those centers about which thine own solar system moves—in Arcturus.

For there had come from those activities, in Uhjltd, the knowledge of the oneness, and of those forces and powers that would set as it were the universality of its relationships, through its unity of purpose in all spheres of human experience; by the entity becoming how? Not aliens, then—not bastards before the Lord—but sons—co-heirs with Him in the Father's kingdom.

Yet the quick return to the earthly sojourn in Troy, and the abuse of these, the turning of these for self—in the activities attempted—brought about the changes that were wrought.

But the entrance into the Ra Ta experience, when there was the journeying from materiality—or the being translated in materiality as Ra Ta—was from the infinity forces, or from the Sun; with those influences that draw upon the planet itself, the earth and all those about same.

Is it any wonder that in the ignorance of the earth the activities of that entity were turned into that influence called the sun worshippers? This was because of the abilities of its influences in the experiences of each individual, and the effect upon those things of the earth in nature itself; because of the atmosphere, the forces as they take form from the vapors created even by same; and the very natures or influences upon vegetation!

The very natures or influences from the elemental forces themselves were drawn in those activities of the elements within the earth, that could give off their vibrations because of the influences that attracted or draw away from one another.

This was produced by that which had come into the experiences in materiality, or into being, as the very nature of water with the sun's rays; or the ruler of thy own little solar system, thy own little nature in the form ye may see in the earth!

Hence we find how, as ye draw your patterns from these, that they become a part of the whole. For ye are *relatively* related to all that ye have contacted in materiality, mentality, spirituality! All of these are a portion of thyself in the material plane.

In taking form they become a mental body with its longings for its home, with right and righteousness.

Then that ye know as thy mental self is the form taken, with all of its variations as combined from the things it has been within, without, and in relationship to the activities in materiality as well as in the spheres or various consciousness of "Have you—love, the circle, the Son?"

These become then as the signs of the entity, and ye may draw these from the pattern which has been set. Just as the desert experience, the lines drawn in the temple as represented by the pyramid, the sun, the water, the well, the sea and the ships upon same—because of the very nature of expression—become the *pattern* of the entity in this material plane.

Draw ye then from that which has been shown ye by the paralleling of thy own experiences in the earth. For they each take their form, their symbol, their sound, their color, their stone. For they all bear a relationship one to another, according to what they have done about, "The Lord is in his holy temple, let all the earth keep silent!"

He that would know his own way, his own relationships to Creative Forces or God, may seek through the promises in Him; as set in Jesus of Nazareth—He passeth by! Will ye have Him enter and sup with thee?

Open then thy heart, thy consciousness, for *He* would tarry with thee! We are through.

Reading 1895-1

The experiences of the entity in the interims of planetary sojourns between the earthly manifestations become the innate mental urges, that may or may not at times be a part of the day dreaming, or the thought and meditation of the inmost self.

Hence we find astrological aspects and influence in the experience, but rather because of the entity's sojourn in the environ than because of a certain star, constellation or even zodiacal sign being in such and such a position at the time of birth.

Know that man—as has been expressed—was given dominion over

all, and in the understanding of same may use all of the laws as pertaining to same for his benefit.

In the application of same as a benefit—if it is for self-indulgence or self-expression alone, it loses its own individuality in the personality of that sought or desired; and thus the very knowledge may be used as a stumbling-stone. But if each experience is as a manifestation to the glory of a creative or heavenly force, or that which is continual thus the judgments being drawn from an ideal that is spiritual in its concept, then there is the greater growth, the greater harmony—for there becomes an at-onement with the influences about same.

Reading 281-55

Q: *Through other planetary sojourns an entity has the opportunity to change its rate of vibration so as to be attracted in the earth plane under another soul number.*

A: Each planetary influence vibrates at a different rate of vibration. An entity entering that influence enters that vibration; not necessary that he change, but it is the grace of God that he may! It is part of the universal consciousness, the universal law.

Reading 1947-1

In giving the urges, then, we find that the astrological influences are not so much because of the certain position of the Sun or the Moon or the Stars, but because of their relationship which is a relativity of influence or force; for, being from the body or materialization, there is the activity of the soul in the environs in which certain influences have been and are accredited to the activities from those planetary sojourns. Thus they become as signs, omens in the experience.

Reading 2599-1

In giving the interpretations of the records as we find them here, these are chosen with the desire and purpose that this be a helpful experience for the entity; enabling it to better fulfill that purpose for which it entered this experience.

Know that one's manifestations in the earth are not by chance but a fulfillment of those purposes the Creative Forces have with each individual entity.

For, the Creative Influence is mindful ever, and hath not willed that any soul should perish, but hath with every temptation prepared a way, a means of escape.

Thus the very fact of a material manifestation should become an awareness to the individual entity of the mindfulness of that influence of Creative Energy in the experience.

Then, as to the abilities with this entity—magnify the virtues, minimize the faults—not only in thy judgments of others. For with what judgment ye mete, it will be meted to thee again.

Thus the purpose of each experience is that the entity may magnify and glorify that which is good. For, good is of the one source, God, and is eternal.

Then as an individual entity magnifies that which is good, and minimizes that which is false, it grows in grace, in knowledge, in understanding.

Know that in the manner ye mete, or do to thy fellow man, so ye do unto thy Maker.

Then let it be from this premise that the judgments and the activities of this entity in this material experience may be drawn as a helpful force in its journey through this particular sojourn.

From the sources of the previous sojourns we find urges arising materially in the experience of the entity—that is, from the previous earthly sojourns as well as the astrological sojourns during the interims between earthly manifestations.

Not that there are influences from the position of stars, planets or the like that may not be met; but these are as urges—just as the environs of an individual in the material plane produce urges, because of studies or activities in a given direction, and because certain material abilities are innately a part of the entity's experience. Yet urges oft arise in the experience of an entity for this or that, the source of which the entity itself may not understand or comprehend—for no one in the family thought or acted in that direction.

Then, this—the environ of the entity, the soul manifesting in the earth—may be called by another name, as with this entity—a part of the present name in the experience before this; and the abilities as an individual to meet others, to influence them in the activities in which certain interests might be magnified, come from the entity's activities in the previous sojourn.

Thus the earthly sojourns make for manifested urges in the present experience. Also those planetary sojourns, in this present solar system, make for urges that are accredited to those particular planets as states of consciousness—that become innately manifested in the present entity.

For instance, in this entity we find the manifestation of Mercury, Venus, Jupiter, Uranus—manifested and latent in the dreams, the visions, the activities; in the high mental abilities of the entity, the ability to reason things through, the stableness of its activity in using not only material but mental forces as an influence to urge others to buy or to be interested in, or to analyze conditions.

Thus in the present, and manifestedly so, the entity might find the abilities as an adjuster, or as an individual to give expression as to evaluation of materials or properties, or abilities of individuals.

In Venus we find that appreciation of the beautiful, as related to art, as related to things, as related to conditions in the relationships of groups of peoples one to another.

Also from Jupiter we find the association with groups, masses, as a reflection in the activities of abilities, and that in which the entity may apply itself in the present experience.

Uranus brings the extremes, in which the entity may rise to great heights of expectation and yet at times find self in a wonderment. Yet innately there are those expectancies in spiritual facts, in the occult, in the psychic forces, that are powers of might for either good or evil. For, as indicated, in Uranus there are the extremes.

Know, as from the first premise, that no influence surpasses the *will* of an individual. The power of will is that birthright as the gift from the Creative Force to each entity, that it may become one with that Influence; knowing itself to be itself yet a part of and one with the Creative Influence as the directing influence in the experience.

Also the earthly sojourns bring urges through the latent faculties of the sensory forces; or they become characteristics that may be indicated—either latent or manifested—as the power or might manifesting; for only as the entity works with or against an influence does it become magnified in the experiences of the entity.

Reading 243-10

In entering, we find, astrologically, the entity coming under the influence of Mercury, Mars, Jupiter, Venus, and Neptune. These, as we find, have builded, and have influenced the entity, in the present experience. Also we find urges as respecting the experiences as related to innate urges, and that as has been *builded* in the present entity.

Aside: Let not this be confusing, as to innate urges and that as is builded in the present experience, for the application of will, and of innate urge through planetary influences, is exercised in this entity as we would find it in few.

In the experience, then, we find these as builded *irrespective* of will, and those that have been builded as respecting the *application* of will's influence; for *will* is that developing factor with which an entity chooses or builds that freedom, or that of being free, knowing the truth as is applicable in the experience, and in the various experiences as has been builded; for that builded must be met, whether in thought or in deed; for thoughts are deeds, and their current run is through the whole of the influence in an ENTITY'S experience. Hence, as was given, "He that hateth his brother has committed as great a sin as he that slayeth a man," for the deed is as of an accomplishment in the mental being, which is the builder for every entity.

Much has been met, much as been *builded* by the entity in the present experience. Much has been experienced by the entity in the various spheres through which the entity has passed.

In that builded, we find one of high, ennobling ideas and ideals; often tempered in Mars, through wrath, that has brought does bring, will bring, many of the experiences that have been experienced in the building of the entity's inner being to the action within the life.

In those influences in Jupiter, finds for the bigness of the entity's vision, the broadness of the good or bad that may be wielded in the influence of those whom the entity contacts from time to time, or period to period, or experience to experience.

In those influences seen in those of Neptune, brings for those of that as is of the *mystery* in the experiences of the entity; the associations in many peculiar circumstances and conditions; the conditions and experiences, and influences, as bring many conditions as, by others, would be misunderstood (and there *be* minds that would misunderstand, rather than know the truth).

In the experiences there has been *innately* built, the fear of evil in the life, the fear of those that would bring condemnation on those who are in power, and oft is the entity too *good* to others for its own good! Through the attempt innate to build that which would be the releasing of those experiences which have been had by the entity.

In those influences seen in Neptune, also brings that water—large *bodies* of water—the entity will gain most through the experience, has gained and will gain, through sojourn near, or passing over, large bodies of water, and *salt* water is preferable; for in the experiences will be seen, fresh hasn't *always* meant for living water.

In those as builded innately, we find:

One that is in that position of making friends easily, and just as easily losing same; yet there are friendships made that make for the better understanding in the experience, and in those of *Venus* forces comes the love that is *innate* in the experience of the entity. Through all the vicissitudes of life this remaineth, for the entity has gained much that makes for that as was given—"There is a friend that sticketh closer than a brother," and "he that is just kind to the least of these, my little ones, is greater than he that hath taken a mighty city." These building, these kept within the consciousness of the entity, will build to that Christ consciousness as makes all free; for in Him is the life, and He is the light that shineth into the dark places, even to the recesses of that of His own consciousness that makes for that which casteth out fear; (for being afraid is the first consciousness of sin's entering in, for he that is made afraid has lost consciousness of self's own heritage with the Son; for we are heirs through Him to that Kingdom that is beyond all that that would make afraid, or that would cause a doubt in the heart of any. Through the recesses of the heart, then, search out that that would make afraid, casting out fear, and *He* alone may guide.)

Editor's Note: The group working with Edgar Cayce attempted to develop tests that would help individuals identify their planetary influences

and their past-life influences. Cayce said that only the astrological was attainable, given that past lives required reading the Akashic Record of a soul or the soul awakening to its memories of past lives. He guided them to use this astrological information for helping to identify one's vocation. Here's that reading:

Text of Reading 5753-3

This Psychic Reading given by Edgar Cayce at his home on Arctic Crescent, Virginia Beach, Va., this 25th day of October, 1939, in accordance with request made by Hugh Lynn Cayce, Manager of the Ass'n for Research & Enlightenment, Inc.

PRESENT

Edgar Cayce; Gertrude Cayce, Conductor; Gladys Davis, Steno. Hugh Lynn Cayce.

READING

Time of Reading 11:30 to 11:40 A.M. Eastern Standard Time.

GC: You will have before you the psychic work of Edgar Cayce relative to information from Life Readings concerning vocational guidance; together with the entity, the enquiring mind, Hugh Lynn Cayce, present here, who seeks to correlate and use such information. From a study of the Life Readings it would seem that an individual's mental and spiritual development, his contentment, is dependent upon releasing and expression of basic mental and emotional urges coming from planetary sojourns and past incarnations. Please give at this time suggestions for the development of a system or a series of intelligence tests which will reveal these basic urges and help an individual in selecting a life's work. It is hoped that such information as may be given here may be developed and used through scout activities and the Princess Anne Schools. You will answer questions.

EC: Yes, we have the information here, that has been indicated in Life Readings as to vocational guidance for individuals.

In developing a plan, or a manner of seeking ways in which individuals might give expression of the latent faculties and powers from the material sojourns, as well as the planetary influences—here we will find that there are conflicting forces and influences at times—as we have indicated.

The astrological aspects may give a tendency, an inclination; and a systematic, scientific study of same would indicate the vocation. And about eighty percent of the individuals would be in the position of being influenced by such astrological aspects; or would be in the position for their abilities to be indicated from same.

But the other twenty percent would not be in that position, due to the influences from activity or the use of their abilities in material experience. Hence in these it would be not only necessary that their material sojourns be given, but as to what had been accomplished through same, and that to be met in the present experience. For, as has been indicated, no influence—astrologically or from material sojourns—surpasses the will or the determination of the individual. Then, there are material factors that rule or govern or direct or influence such forces. These may be tempered by the astrological aspects, but these are not (the astrological aspects) the major influence or force—the will.

Thus, only about eighty percent of the individuals may have their abilities indicated from the astrological aspects in the direction of vocational guidance, as to be a determining factor for such.

If some five individuals would be taken, and their charts or astrological aspects indicated, and questions asked as to determining the influence or force from same—from such an aspect there might be given information so that a general chart might be indicated for a questionnaire, or a test, or an activity that would be of material benefit in a great *number* of individuals—but never a perfect score may be indicated. For the will, as well as the factors of environment, have their influence.

Ready for questions.

Q: *How can the urges from past incarnations be determined by a test or series of tests?*

A: As just indicated—this may only be done by giving the material sojourns of the individual.

But if the astrological aspects and influences are given, then there may be determined a questionnaire from same.

Q: *Should the chart be drawn from the geocentric or the heliocentric system?*

A: The geocentric system would be the more in keeping with the Persian force or influence.

Q: *Any other suggestion to Hugh Lynn Cayce regarding the development of this at this time?*

A: As indicated, there may be charts drawn of five individuals, and a questionnaire may be determined for factors in the individual experience—as to what their inclinations or activities are. Not by telling, but by questioning!

Then *from* same, as indicated, there may be given a more correct or direct questionnaire that would be helpful for a large *number* of individuals—but *not* a perfect score.

For in about twenty percent of the populace at the present time, it is dependent upon what the individuals have done with their urges *through* material sojourns.

As indicated trough this channel, some are in keeping with the astrological charts, others are found to be partially so, others are diametrically opposed to same—because of the activities of the individuals.

We are through for the present.

Editor's Note: Cayce's discourses state that all souls were created at the same moment, yet Cayce used the term "old soul" occasionally. He later explained that he meant a soul that has been sojourning in and around the earth for many lifetimes. The following is a reading for an old soul, and this reading has many interesting references to planetary and constellational sojourning.

Text of Reading 436-2 M 28
(Elevator Boy, Christian with East Indian leaning)

This psychic reading given by Edgar Cayce at Lillian Edgerton, Inc., 267 Fifth Ave., N.Y.C., this 10th day of November, 1933, in accordance with request made by self—Mr. [436], Active Member of the Ass'n for Research & Enlightenment, Inc.

PRESENT

Edgar Cayce; Hugh Lynn Cayce, Conductor; Gladys Davis, Steno. Mr. [436].

READING

Born March 29, 1905, (11:30 P.M.) in Midland, Virginia.

Time of Reading 3:00 to 3:50 P.M. Eastern Standard Time
. . . . , D.C.

(Life Reading Suggestion)

EC: Yes, we have the entity and those relations with the universe and universal forces, that are latent and exhibited in the personalities of the present entity, [436].

It would be well to comment upon the oldness of this soul, especially in its activities—as will be seen—in periods when the occult and mystic influences were manifested in the experience of the entity in the earth; and make for influences that have been (or may be made) very good or very bad in the experience of the entity. Hence, this is an old soul.

In giving the personalities and the individuality of the entity in the present experience, we must approach same from the astrological, though these in the very fact of that given respecting its activities in the earth during such periods when such changes or activities were manifested in the material affairs of individuals, make for little that may be compulsory in astrological influence. Yet *impulses* arise from these influences.

As in passing from Pisces into Aries, there are those influences innately and manifested in the mental forces of the body; much of both of these, and they become conflicting in the experience at times of the entity.

Pisces brings rather the mystery and creative forces, and magnanimous aspects in students of—or in the thought of—influences in the active principles of individual impulse; with Aries bringing reason, or air, or airy actions, yet reason, more than Pisces would make the demands in the self at time for reasons for every manifestation, whether material conditions, mental or spiritual conditions in the experience of the entity. And at other periods it may be said that the entity becomes rather susceptible to influences about the body, without considering seriously the sources of the information and as to whether same is able to be verified by others or not. Feelings of same impress the entity from this astrological influence, which—as we see—does not only control earth's sojourn but the position of the entity in this sojourn through the planetary influences in the earth's solar system.

As to the sojourns in the astrological influences then, we find these are the ruling; not from their position at the birth, but rather from the position of the entity's activities in that environ.

Mars is an influence rather from the associations then, in self's own experience. Or when dissensions, distrust, dissatisfaction, madness, wars, arise; these come *about* the entity rather than influencing the *activities* of the entity, other than through the associations with individuals that make demands upon the entity and its activities in these directions. These become at times concrete experiences in the entity's activities in the present experience; yet these, as we find, for many a year now (and these began some three years ago) will be less in the experience until Mars in '38 or '39 becomes nearer in its influence upon the sojourners of those in the earth that have experienced a sojourn in that environ.

Hence this may be said, in a manner, to be of little influence then in the period, or during that period, when the entity should make for a stabilization in self's experience of that to which it may develop its better abilities in this present sojourn in the earth.

From Venus rather a complex position or condition comes to the experience of the entity, where filial or marital or such relations as of loves in the material earth come in the experience. Not that there hasn't been, nor won't be, nor isn't existent, that which is pure, elevating and helpful in the experience of the entity in its relationships with individuals of both sexes in this way and manner; yet these have brought some very pleasant experiences and some very contrary and contradictory influences in the activities and in the experience of the entity in the present.

Hence it may be given in passing, to the entity, that the love of and for a pure body is the most sacred experience in an entity's earth sojourn; yet these conditions soured, these conditions turned into vitrol, may become the torments of an exemplary body, and one well-meaning, and make for loss of purposes.

Keep the friendships, then. Keep those relationships that are founded upon all that is constructive in earth, in the mind, in the spirit.

As to those influences from the sojourn of the entity in Uranian

forces, as may be indicated from that given as to the oldness and as to
the delving into the occult and mystic and the application in the experience, the entity has sojourned more than once in this environ and
under quite varied or different experiences and manifestations. Hence
there are periods when earthly conditions, mental conditions, spiritual
conditions, are very good; and others when all are very bad in the
experience of the entity in the present. Yet, as we find, in the application
of self as related to the impulses that may rise in the consciousness of
the entity in the present experience from those impulses received from
the sojourns, these may be made the strong fort in the activities of self
in the present. But they must be tempered, from the very experiences in
the sojourn, to making for not an active force in those experiences from
planetary influences in a weak body, but turn to strengthening the
body–physical for the manifestations of the correct raising of those vital
energies in the material body, through which such influences may make
for manifestations and experiences in the earth's sojourn. These influences from Uranus make for many of the ills that have been in the
experience in the body, in the nervous reactions to the physical body,
to the weak experiences to the physical body, when the very vital life
force of a material body was in danger of being separated from physical
for an ethereal sojourn.

As to the appearances, then, and their influence in the present, these
are given as the ones influencing the activities of the present body;
rather than numbers, we give those that make for the greater activity in
the present:

Before this we find the entity was in the land of nativity, and about
those places, those peoples, where the first settlings were—and the first
sojournings that spread beyond the mere force builded; or about that
town that was the first capitol of this new land, or this portion of same.
And among the activities there are many of those things being recon-
structed, re–enacted, that will be not only of physical interest but will,
with the application of the abilities within self, recall to the entity many
of the associations that the entity had with the peoples of the land
(native). While the entity did not go what is proverbially called "native"
in the experience, the associations were such, with those that acted in
the capacity of the spiritual leaders (or with what were termed the medi-

cine men of the period), and with those that later attempted to set themselves as leaders of this people, that the entity made friends both with the natives and the colonists, aiding the colonists in the period to establish better relations; in the name then Edward Compton, a distant family name even that may be found among those that sojourned in the peninsula land of that portion of the country.

The entity lost and gained through the experience; gained in the application of self for the benefiting of those with whom the entity sojourned, and the natives also whom the entity aided in making better cooperative relationships in the activities of the people of the period and time. The entity aided in establishing such relationships that there was the trading of the native peoples in distant lands. One particular period of interest, that may be noted in history, was when the entity aided in bringing to the peoples corn from the western portion of their native land, that sustained those peoples through a very bad period.

From that period there is the influence oft in the present in those activities when studies of those peoples are the experience of the entity, and there are both confusing and constructive influences. Yet, when about many of a mediumistic turn, many of those with whom the entity engaged in life and activity would attempt to speak to the entity; especially one that termed himself Big Rock, Black Rock.

Before this we find the entity was during that period when there were the returnings of those peoples in the land now called Greece, from the rebellions that had been active in Mesopotamia and in the regions about what is known as Turkey and those lands; during those periods of Xenophon's activities and those wars.

The entity was among the few of these natives, strong in body, purposeful in intent, to return to the native land; and the entity gained through the experience but lost in the latter portion of the sojourn when returning to the native land, when power was entrusted in the activities of the entity; and while the purposefulness was correct, there arose those that distrusted and brought contentions by the accusations brought against the entity, in the name Xerxion. Then Xerxion lost in faith in his fellow man, and the faith in the purposefulness of those that were attributing to the gods, or the powers and forces as they were named and termed, the elements to maintain the equilibrium. Hence in that the entity lost, and in the present—while there are those abilities in self to lead for a purposefulness in its activity, too oft has the entity become discouraged when accusations of unkind things were brought, or when experiences made for the losing of confidences in friends and associates it has made discouragements too easily in the experience in the present. This (in passing, may be said) is a test period for the entity in its relationship, particularly. Hence the entity should turn to the abilities within and find self first, knowing in what, in whom the entity has believed; knowing He is able to keep that which is committed unto Him against any experience that may arise in the lives or activities of those who are His loved ones, His chosen. Who has He chosen? They that do His biddings. What are His biddings? Love the Lord thy God with all thine heart (and thy God meaning Him that in Spirit is the Creative Forces of all that is manifested), keeping self unspotted from the world or any smirch of activity, and loving thy neighbor, thy brother, as thine self. These will make for the relieving of all those influences in the experience, and bring harmony, peace, joy, understanding, in the experience of the entity; and will enable the entity to not only study, not only to understand, but—best of all—to comprehend from what source many of those influences arise, as we will see has to do upon the mental body of the entity, and become active oft in the physical forces or the physical activities through their nerve reflexes in a material body.

Before this we find the entity was in that land now known as the Egyptian, during that period when there was the returning of those that had been astrayed through the sending away of the priest of the land.

The entity was among those that were banished with the priest, being with the priest Ra Ta in the association and in the activities of gathering together the tenets that the scribe—in a way; rather the one gathering the data than one scribing or protecting the data—collected. The entity aided the priest specifically in some of the associations and connections with those of the temple gatherers to whom the priest gave heart and mind; and for the act among those the entity was severely punished when banished by the natives, rather than the king. Yet, being healed by the priest in the foreign land, the entity came again into Egypt when there was the re-establishing, and aided in rebuilding the temples of service; being active then in what today would be called the preparations for those things that kept the cleansings of the temple after use of individual in body, or as a caretaker (termed in the present) of offices, temples, churches or buildings. Then the entity was in the name Pth-Lerr. The entity gained and gained, and much that is suffered in body is as a bringing to bear of that which may make the mental contact with the tenets of the experience.

One might ask (this aside, please), why would such be brought to bear? Because, with the experience of the entity in the period, seeing the developments and the activities, there was set within the soul that desire: "Come what may, whatever is necessary in my whole experience of my soul, make me to know again the joys of the tenets of Ra Ta."

In the present these may mean much, if they are builded for a soul development in the present; for these needs be to overcome those experiences in the sojourn just previous in the Atlantean land.

Before this we find the entity in the Atlantean land rather rebelled with those forces of Baalilal, with those activities in the electrical appliances, when these were used by those peoples to make for beautiful buildings without but temples of sin within.

The entity, in the name Saail, was a priest (demoted) in the Temple of Oz in Atlantis, and lost from soul development, gained from material things; yet these fade, these make raids upon the body in physical manifestations. These make for hindrances in activity in that known within the innate self. For, rather were the mysteries of the black arts as applied in the experience practiced by Saail, yet these in the present may be turned into account in material things in making material connections; but use or apply same in the experience rather in the mental and spiritual manner for the soul development of the entity, rather than for materiality in the present. These are weaknesses, then, yet weakness is only strength misapplied or used in vain ways.

Before this we find the entity was in that land that has been termed Zu, or Lemuria, or Mu. This was before the sojourn of peoples in perfect body form; rather when they may be said to have been able to—through those developments of the period—be in the body or out of the body and act upon materiality. In the spirit or in flesh these made those things, those influences, that brought destruction; for the atmospheric pressure in the earth in the period was quite different from that experienced by the physical being of today.

The entity then was in the name Mmuum, or rather those calls that make easy the mysteries of words as related to sounds and rote that bring to the consciousness, in those that have indwelled in those lands, that activity that merits (not the word), that brings, that impulse that urges that those forces from without act upon the elements in whatever sphere they may bring a material manifestation. This must be controlled within self, from those influences in [436]; for these are those things at times that hinder.

Let self, then, be grounded rather in the faith of that which is, was, and ever will be, the source of all spirit, all thought all mind, all physical manifestation—the *one* God, as called in this period. In that period he was called Zu-u-u-u-u; in the next Ohm—Oh-u-m; in the next (now known as Egypt) with Ra Ta, He was called God—G-o-r-r-d!

As to the abilities of the entity, and that to which it may attain, and how, in the present:

First it may be said, study—through that known in self of the spiritual and mental forces active in the experience of the body—to show self approved unto an ideal that is set in the Son, the Christ, knowing that in possessing the consciousness of His love, His manifestation, all is well; for, as is known, without that love as He manifested among men, nothing can, nothing did, nothing will come into consciousness of matter. Not that we may deny evil and banish it, but supplanting and rooting out evil in the experience, replacing same with the love that is in the consciousness of the body Jesus, the Christ, we may do all things in His name; and using those opportunities in whatsoever sphere of activity the entity may find to show forth those commands He gave, "If ye love me, keep my commandments." What, ye ask, are His commandments? "A new commandment give I unto you, that ye love one another." What, then, are the fruits of love? The fruits of the spirit; which are kindness, hope, fellowship, brotherly love, friendship, patience; these are the fruits of the spirit; these are the commands of Him that ye manifest them in whatsoever place ye find yourself, and your soul shall grow in grace, in knowledge, in understanding, and that joy that comes with a perfect knowledge in Him brings the joys of earth, the joys of the mental mind, or joys of the spheres, and the *glory* of the Father in thine experience.

Ready for questions.

Q: When will adverse planetary change for better influences in my life?

A: As indicated, the receding of Mars brings, and has brought, better planetary influences; as the mental activities and applications in the light of the love in Christ brings with those activities in the coming closer and closer of Venus with Uranus; which begins in December, present year, for the approach, reaching nearer conjunction in May or June of the coming year better conditions, mentally, materially, financially.

Q: What is the main purpose of this incarnation?

A: To set self aright as respecting the variations in those tenets in the first two experiences in the sojourn, tempered in those tenets given in Ra Ta—that, "The Lord Thy God is *one!*" And manifesting of that oneness in the little things makes the soul grow in His grace!

We are through for the present.

Editor's Note: Cayce even gave readings on how to subdue negative influences from planetary or astrological soul activity. Here's one example:

Text of Reading 137-18 M 27
(Stockbroker, Jewish)

This psychic reading given by Edgar Cayce at his office, 322 Grafton Avenue, Dayton, Ohio, this 24th day of July, 1925, in accordance with request made by self—Mr. [137].

PRESENT

Edgar Cayce; Mrs. Cayce, Conductor; Gladys Davis, Steno.

READING

Born October 28, 1898, in New York City. On the floor of Time of Reading the New York Stock 9:30 A.M. Dayton Savings Time. Exchange, Wall & New Streets, N.Y.

GC: You will have before you the body of [137], on the floor of the N.Y. Stock Exchange, Wall and New Streets, New York City, N.Y., with the information as has been given this body in readings given for same on the 28th day of October, 1924, also that given on the 12th day of Janu-

ary, 1925, [See 137-4 and 137-12] especially that portion of same relating
to the undue influences in the life of [137] when Moon's forces square to
Saturn and Mars bring doubts within the body's mental forces. This is
given in reading of January 12th, as occurring in the week of August 13,
1925. You will please tell us just the character of influence that will
occur, whether of mental, spiritual or physical forces, and how this entity may guard against this influence.

EC: Yes, we have the body here, and the information as has been
given this body in regards to influences as are exercised in the life of
the entity at the periods given, through position of the planetary forces
as are exercised in the life of same.

Now, we find that with the indwelling urges as are seen within the
individual, when there occur certain positions of those planetary influences under which the body (meaning spiritual force body) has developed, these bring the intense urge towards those experiences of the
entity as it passed through that phase of its development, for we find
the urge within each entity is its experiences in all phases of its existence, plus the environmental conditions of body at time, with the will
of entity counterbalancing same through body–mind urge. Hence the
necessity of each entity understanding, having knowledge of those laws
that do govern same in the material or physical realm, as well as those
pertaining to the spiritual forces as are manifest through the body in
each of its various changes, for we find all are one, for the real body is
that spiritual force manifesting in same, always through the Trinity of
that comprising same.

In the information as has been given as we find, these influences
come for this body at this particular or special time, when through the
influences as are exercised in the position Moon, Jupiter, with Saturn
and with Mars, this brings to that body, [137], those of that urge, that
doubt of self and self's abilities to manifest either mental (Moon with
Saturn), with physical, (doubting of own physical health, see?) through
the forces or powers in Mars, the own spiritual forces as is the influence,
or undue influence on Jupiter's forces with this position as manifested.
Then, we find these at this time pertaining to this nature:

The body–mind, the spiritual–mind, has reached at this period, especially, and during week of August 13, 1925, that place where the doubts

of every nature, pertaining to this threefold force as is given here, come to the body. Hence, we will find, will be easily aggravated through any mental association, whether in business relation, moral relations socially or marital relations, for, seemingly, at this time would occur all of these combining with one to bring the detrimental forces to the mind. With the condition of mind comes that condition where the physical forces, apparently, respond more to these of the conditions wherein weaknesses are shown or manifested in same. Then the combination of all would bring as to that—well—"I don't care! What difference does it make? Let it go to pot!"—See?

Then, to overcome this, rather place those forces as are manifest through will forces, knowing that these do appear. That, "Get thee behind me Saturn (Satan), that I *will* serve the living God, with *my* body, *my* mind, *my* money, *my* spirit, *my* soul, for I and *His*, and through *me*, my body, my mind, do I manifest *my* impression, *my* interpretation of *my* God."

This does, not, as we see, relate to physical accidents, physical conditions, physical things, pertaining to the material things of life, save as would be affected by same through—"Well, I don't care."

We are through for the present.

4

●

Reincarnation Unnecessary: Breaking Free of the Wheel of Karma and Reincarnation

Editor's Note: About twelve hundred people received "life readings" from Edgar Cayce. Life readings are those in which Cayce gave people's past lives, explaining how these previous incarnations affected the present life. Of these many life readings, eighteen people were told that this present incarnation may be their *last*, indicating that there was no longer any compelling force or karmic pull necessitating another incarnation on earth. These following readings reveal some of the reasons why these people would not have to reincarnate.

My colleagues and I knew some of these people, and we can assure you that they were not perfect. In fact, they had many common human weaknesses. Some of them also had very difficult lives, with much sorrow and suffering. Others had fairly normal lives, with no outstanding quality that we could point to as the reason for their breakthrough to life beyond incarnation on earth.

Apparently, their freedom from the wheel of karma and reincarnation occurred *within* themselves, in their hearts and minds, because there are little to no outward reasons for their release from the cycle of incarnations. One part of their stories that was common among them is that this last incarnation was the culmination of *many* incarnations that led up to this opportunity. Even though this was their last incarnation, they were told that they had the freedom to return if they desired, but they no longer had to.

The following are the life readings for ten of the eighteen souls for whom reincarnation became unnecessary.

1. Case #987
Editor's Note: In this first case, Cayce begins with this statement: "The entity may complete its earth's experience in the present, if it so chooses."

Text of Reading 987-2 F 47
(Housewife, Christian)

This psychic reading given by Edgar Cayce at his home on Arctic Crescent, Virginia Beach, Va., this 9th day of August, 1935, in accordance with request made by the self—Mrs. [987], Associate Member of the Ass'n for Research & Enlightenment, Inc., via Mr. [257] and Mrs. [903].

PRESENT

Edgar Cayce; Gertrude Cayce, Conductor; Gladys Davis, Steno. Mrs. [987].

READING

Born December 27, 1887, in Northville, Michigan.

Time of Reading 3:50 to 4:50 P.M. Eastern Standard Time. New York City.

(Life Reading Suggestion)

EC: Yes, we have the entity and those relations with the universe and universal forces; that are latent and manifested in the personalities of the entity now known as or called [987].

A golden cord runs through the astrological, the numerological and the earth's experiences of this entity. The entity may complete its earth's experience in the present, if it so chooses.

Then, in giving that which may be helpful or beneficial to the entity in making application of those things that have and do become a part of its present experience, it is well that much that may be given be kept, be presented to others, that they, too, may take hope, may know there is *still* that hope in the *living* of those influences, those creative energies that bring into the experiences of man the knowledge of the at-oneness with that Creative Force, that Mighty I AM Presence that exists, which the Giver of the good gifts has given to all.

We find that the astrological influences have very little to do with this entity, yet may be seen as urges in the experience and how the entity has applied those urges in the material manifestations of same.

For all in matter, all in form, first began in the urge of the mental or the spiritual influence, that *prompted* same to come into manifestations under the influence of a guiding hand.

In the entity we find that Jupiter is the ruling force, with Venus; which combination makes for beauty of attainment and the longing—as it is the experience of the entity—to present to others that phase, that part of the experience that is beautiful, that is better. Not to exaggeration, but rather as the entity has experienced that which is of error, that which is of shame, that which is of disrupting forces, becomes negligible unless given power by the thought, by the activity on the part of some mind. Not that denying alone makes for non-existence, but rather that those things presenting themselves as errors, as a faux pas, as a disrupting influence, may be used as the stepping-stones for the creating of those atmospheres, those environs in which each and every soul may find in a trial, in a temptation, in a hardship even, that of beauty. For through the things which He suffered He became the King of kings, the Lord of lords. So in man, that has named a Name that is above every name, it is found that with the using of experiences there may be brought into his consciousness that harmony, which is another name for peace, another name for good, another name for joy, which will be crowned in glory.

In the urge arising from these influences we find that there is the necessity for the entity to learn a little more of Patience. For Selfishness is not a portion of the entity's own being; rather is it the lack of the Patience; not with others but the more with self. For as He gave, it is in patience that ye become aware of thy soul!

So in its associations with others the entity needs to forget those things that have made for hardships, that have made for misunderstandings in relationships as one to another—whether with individuals or with groups; though the entity may find oft that it requires that self turn within, that the consciousness of His Presence abiding may direct. Thus may there be brought peace and patience, as an *active* force; not as a passive influence in the experience of self but as an *active* influence!

This has brought into self that association where tolerance has not *always* been felt, as may be seen through the appearances of the entity in the earth; not tolerance as a passive thing but tolerance as an active force! For while each soul, each expression may have the right of its own opinion and its own activity, it should not only say so but act in such a manner; knowing that each soul is destined to become a portion again of the First Cause, or back to its Maker. And as there is the awareness of its individuality, its ability to apply its portion, the *soul*-portion of the Creative Forces or Energies or God within itself, it builds that in a soul-body which may be One with that Creative Force.

For while flesh and blood that is of the earth–earthy may not gain or know glory, the body—the *real* body; not the superficial but the *real* body—may become aware of its presence in the Presence of the body of God and among its brethren, and a portion of that Whole.

So does there become the awareness of tolerance in faith, that is the activity of this entity in the present, to become that which may make the ability in the entity or soul experience to use that *in hand* as the influences for such an awareness that the body-soul may not need to know flesh save as it chooses same for its own missions for that Creative Energy.

In Jupiter we find the influences making for abilities of specific natures in the experience of the entity; as in constructive thinking for individuals and for groups, whether this be for writing or for instruction in this or that form. It will find that in the application of self there may be much given to others, in the form of papers, in the form of charts, in the form of instruction that may become—as it were—a light set on a hill for many who grope in darkness and in doubt, who are fearful. For that quieting through the gaining of patience in self may enable the entity to give that light and that instruction necessary for the guiding of many.

Venus makes for close friendships with those whom the entity finds in its experience; not only as a great love for its fellow man but in making for ties that hold, of the spirit rather than of the flesh. Hence kindred souls in all walks of life may find in associations with the entity much that becomes as a complement, as a helpment [helper? helpmate? helpmeet?] to their own struggles. This is expressed in a truth He gave: "Who is my brother? Who is my mother? Who is my sister? They that do the will of my father in heaven, the same are my mother, my brother, my sister."

This is the love that all should come to know, even as it has been attained in a great measure by this entity through the experiences it has gained in its sojourns. And more and more will the entity become aware of same in *active* tolerance and *active* patience.

In Uranus we find the extremist influences, that have been experienced by the entity in the present and that come as urges in the experiences day by day. Oft, from that sojourn or environ in the Uranian experience, does the entity find itself *impelled*—as it were—to do this or that; which may be entirely at variance to what reason or cold reason would tell the entity. And it makes for those experiences with its friendships, or a certain portion of same, wherein the entity seems to be—or appears to others to be—*somewhat* peculiar or odd in its choice of this or that activity in relationships to its associations, its reading, its study, its line of endeavor in this or that manner of recreation.

All of these become a portion of the entity's urge and experience; as does also the interest in things that are psychic or occult or mystic, these have a part in the urges in the experience of the entity. Hence mystical signs, mystical numbers, mystical conditions have much to do with the entity at times. And these may come in the *vision* and in the dreams (that have been for the time set aside), more and more as the entity turns to those *patience* applications.

For, as will be seen, the entity made *for* the priest the Urim and the Thummim!

And the entity may give much of that which comes as an influence in the experiences through the deeper meditation; much constructive counsel to those that seek into the mysteries that are hidden in the activities of those who would give their expression of that they have conceived from the Spirit, that *motivates* them in their activities.

Then, in these do we find the greater influences from the astrological sojourns.

As to the appearances in the earth and those that influence the entity in the present, we find—while far apart in their activity—these have been those that bring to the entity much of the urges that arise through the emotional nature of the entity in *this present* manifestation, or materialization:

Before this we find the entity was in the land of the present nativity, but in and about that known as the Vinland [Vineland. In reading 261-21, he gave the correct location as now 987-2 Salem, Mass., then all of what is now Cape Cod area, Providence and Newport, Rhode Island] or about Provincetown and Salem, during the early periods of those activities when the persecutions arose for those who heard the unusual, who experienced the moving of an influence or force from without themselves.

The *entity* then was close to many of those who were beset by such experiences; hearing, knowing, experiencing many sides of the material manifestations; hearing and knowing many sides of the influences in the experiences of those that *had* the meetings and were acquainted with such activities.

Then the entity was close to, and the companion of, the minister in the Salem activity; one Nancy Donnelly.

In the experience the entity gained; yet those things that made for the fear of material suffering, the fear of what people said in criticism, builded much that was hard to be borne in the experience of the entity during that sojourn. Yet the entity, it may be said, gained in the mental and spiritual experience; and has brought to this present sojourn that influence wherein the entity hears much that others would say or would give of their activity, of their experience, and has judged oft well, has judged oft according to those experiences as the minister's helper.

This is a portion that must be met in that activity of tolerance, in that active patience in self.

The abilities from that sojourn are towards the setting down of data pertaining to the intricate activities or details of an experience; these become a portion of the entity in its greater activity.

The entity's social life, its marital life, its relations with its blood *in* the present have arisen much from those experiences.

The weirdness of Salem, also the weirdness of the vault or any of those places wherein the dead have buried their dead, finds a gloom within the entity's experience. Yet those places of beauty where there is honor for memory, the trust is in the living God, bring an uplifting in the inmost being of the entity. These are from those experiences, as it heard the sound of those calls during that Provincetown period.

Before that we find the entity was in the land now known as the Persian or Arabian, when there were the gatherings of many to the city in the hills and in the plains.

The entity was of those Persian peoples, or the first of the Croesus'; being in the relations to or in the household of the king.

And as there came to be the greater understanding of the tenets and truths given by the teacher Uhjltd, that brought not only health in body but a balance in the mental minds of those that came to the city in the plains for instructive forces, the entity was one who rose to the position of the Princess after the destruction of the king's daughter in the raid.

Then the entity rose to power, through the healing that was brought in the body from the leader in the tented city.

And as it made application of those tenets, as it gathered those of its own household and of its own kingdom for the profession and application of those things that had been gathered from the teacher, much came to the entity and to the surroundings of same, in power, in glory, in the beautiful things that were builded in that land.

From that experience in the present the entity finds that those things oriental, those things pertaining to the Persian plaids and Persian silks, those brocaded conditions that were made by many of the entity's associates for their helpfulness in bringing beauty to those peoples, become—as it were—an influence in the entity's present experience.

And those tenets held as we have indicated will make for harmonious experience and the joy of same; as do certain sounds of music, certain sounds of chant, certain sounds of activity, bring to the entity an awakening and a consciousness of a movement from within that awakens something as the entity experienced during that sojourn.

Before that we find the entity was in that land, that period, when the chosen people were being given upon the holy mount the manner of their exercise in the temple, or in the service before the tabernacle.

The entity then was among the daughters of Levi, and those chosen to make the vestment of the priest. And to the entity, because of its own abilities, there was given the preparation of the settings of the breastplate and the putting of the stones thereon, and the preparation of the Urim and Thummim for the interpretations of the movements that came upon the high priest in the holy of holies to be given to his people in or from the door of the tabernacle.

Then in the name Henriettah, the entity's activities were in a high force *equal to* the cousin, Miriam.

Throughout the experience the entity gained; for it reasoned with Nadab and Abihu; it counseled for Korah, yet did not allow self to become entangled in any of those influences that would have made for the rise to the position of fame. Rather did the entity choose to remain as one in the background that there might be given the greater understanding to that mighty people as they stood in the presence of the I AM that had brought them to the holy mount.

In the present from that sojourn, those things pertaining to the mysteries of the temple, the mysteries of numbers, of figures, and those things that have their hidden meaning, become as a portion of the entity. Yet oft does there arise that sudden change as to the fearfulness of people giving too great a power to such things that would lead them astray; as they did in the experience of the entity in the wilderness.

Before that we find the entity was in the land now known as the Indian and Egyptian, during those periods when there were the gatherings of those from many of the lands for the correlating of the truths that were presented by Saneid in the Indian land, by Ra Ta in the Egyptian land, by Ajax from the Atlantean land, by those from the Carpathian land, by those from the Pyrenees, by those from the Incal and those from the Oz lands, and by those from that activity which will again be uncovered in the Gobi land.

And *here* the entity may find a great interest, a great power, in the instructions and help that it may land to others in their choosing the places of seeking for that knowledge that may make for a more universality of thought *throughout* the universe in spiritual lines.

Then the entity was among the natives of the Egyptian land, and rose to power through those cleansings in the Temple of Sacrifice; then becoming a portion of the activative service in the Temple Beautiful when it made for those abilities within self to mete out to many those things necessary in their physical and mental understanding.

And with the correlating of the thought, the entity became first as the representative of the Temple Beautiful in the Indian land; and later—and during the period of its greatest height—in the land of the Gobi, or the Mongoloid. *There* the entity was as the priestess in the Temple of Gold, which is still intact there.

The entity then, as Shu-shent, made for great development; and from those experiences in the present comes the abilities for the teachings, for the ministering, for the leading of many.

As to the abilities of the entity in the present (though much more might be given, especially of the activities of the entity as Shu-shent—for they were many), we find this is the activity necessary:

Keep that faith thou *innately* hast in the *oneness* of power in the Creative Forces as it makes for manifestations in the hearts and minds of men; and as ye do it in thy activities with thy fellow man, as ye do it in thy meditation, as ye do it in thy mind, so will it be meted to thee in thine inner self. For all must pass under the *rod*; but He has tempered this with mercy and judgment. So must ye temper thine judgments, so must ye find thy patience, so must ye find those things within self that make for the answer of thyself before the Throne of grace. For if ye would have mercy ye must show mercy to thy fellow man; yea to thine very enemy, to those that despitefully use you. Laugh with those who laugh; mourn with those who mourn, in the Lord. *Keep* thy paths straight, and ye will find *glory—glory*—unto thyself!

In the writing of books, in the ministry of tracts or tenets that may be helpful in song, in verse; in these are thy activities. But forsake not thy faith in the *oneness* of Truth!

Ready for questions.

Q: Have I an inferiority complex, and what can I do to overcome it?

A: As we have indicated, through the urge from the Uranian influence we find experiences that make for individuals speaking so as to make the entity conscious that it has acted quickly without thought; that it has acted quickly by an urge from within; but not an inferiority complex. Rather is there the necessity, as we have indicated, to meet such experiences with patience; and to have *tolerance* with those that misjudge. For say oft, "They know not what they do!"

Q: What am I best fitted for, to make my life more interesting in the way of accomplishment?

A: As indicated in the preparation of tracts, in the preparation of data, in the preparation of songs, of music, in the preparation of rhythmical movements for those who are seeking. For it may be said of this entity as of very few, that in such preparations it would never allow those using same to lose sight of the oneness of power. And so few there be who write or meditate, or who give formulas for others, that do not let the *formula* become the power *rather* than the influence being sought!

Q: How can my husband [1021] be influenced to develop his spiritual nature?

A: Not by might nor by power, but "by my word, saith the Lord of hosts!" Be patient, be kind, be gentle. A hint here, an understanding there; add little by little will it be seen that the little leaven leaveneth the whole lump. Not my might would thou cause him to do this or that, but let thy activities and thy word be of such a nature, such a character, that they *impel*—by the desire to be more and more in a oneness of accord with those in thine own surroundings.

Q: How can I improve memory and concentration?

A: Study well that which has been given through these sources on Meditation. Through meditation may the greater help be gained. As it has been indicated oft to the body, *do it* and leave the results to the Creative Forces; for they are a part of thee. Let thy light so shine (for thou hast gone far on the highway) that others, seeing, may take hope and find that song, too, that springs oft within thy breast.

We are through for the present.

2. Case #569

Editor's Note: In this next life reading, Cayce gives much detail and guidance, then calmly ends the reading with this statement: "Through thy own efforts in self there need not be the necessity in returning to earth's plane."

Text of Reading 569-6 F 45
(Housekeeper, Protestant)

This Psychic Reading given by Edgar Cayce at his office, 115

West 35th Street, Virginia Beach, Va., this 29th day of November, 1925, in accordance with request made by self—Miss [569], via her step-cousin, Mrs. [538] [they were brought up in same household like sisters].

PRESENT

Edgar Cayce; Mrs. Cayce, Conductor; Gladys Davis, Steno. Hugh Lynn Cayce.

READING

Born May 6, 1880, in Mascoutah, Illinois.

Time of Reading 2:45 P.M. Eastern Standard Time. . . . , Ky.

GC: You will have before you [569], who was born May 6, 1880, in Mascoutah, Illinois, and you will give the relation of this entity and the Universe, and the Universal Forces, giving the conditions that are as personalities, latent and exhibited, in the present life. Also the former appearances in the earth's plane, giving time, place, and the name, and that in that life which built or retarded the development for the entity, giving the abilities of the present entity and to that which it may attain, and how.

EC: Yes, we have the entity here, and those relations with the Universal Forces as are manifested in the present sphere. Also those relations with the Universal Forces as are latent in the personality of the entity, with those conditions as do appear from the entrances into the earth's plane, and those influences in the present individuality of the entity.

In taking the position in the present earth's plane, we find under the influence of Jupiter and Venus, with Mercury and Uranus in the distance. In the adverse influence then of Vulcan and of the Pleiades. Hence the conditions as have to do with the relations in the present earth's sphere.

As to the personality as is exhibited in the present earth plane, we find one ever given to those ennobling influences in Jupiter and in Venus. Then with love, with prudence, with truth, with all of those classifications of those virtues as are found in the relation of Venus and Jupiter. See, there's a whole lot of money due the body that it has never gotten [2/22/26 letter thanking EC for 569-7: "When you find that 'whole lot of money' that is due me I'm going to pay you well for your trouble and kindness to me."], and with the influences then in the life, there is brought these conditions as the latent forces in the urges of entity:

One that is considered peculiar by many, in its action, in its thought. One that is in the influence of love's forces ever. One that is lover of nature, of developing nature in every way, in the beauties in nature, in flowers [3/19/26 EC wrote saying he'd appreciate her sending him the flower seeds she promised for his flower boxes.], in music, in art, in every nature of the studies and the spirit as is manifest in same, and we shall see from the position many of these urges are taken.

One that may give much joy to many peoples, always giving, giving, more than ever receiving.

As to the appearances:

In the one before this we find in France, in the days when the Second Charles was in exile. The entity then in the name of Asada, and in the household of those [including [538]] who sheltered the escaped man or ruler afterwards, and assisted in the keeping of soldiery from capturing same, and was ever a favorite of that ruler, and the latter days were spent in the foreign port from birth, in England, see? and the urges as seen, the particular care in dress, and ability to keep secrets more than ordinary.

In the one before this we find in the Persian rule, when the forces were being over-run by the Grecians, and the entity then [was] carried as one of the captives to that country [period of Uhjltd], being then in the name Aurial, and in the household of the friend to the one who afterward gave much of the first philosophy of faith to this people, yet being persecuted for that belief and action. In this we find the entity as Aurial developed much, and gained much in the knowledge of the mental developments as were seen in the human forces. The urges as we see in the present from this, when once set in mind as to purpose or intent, hard to change, for that innate feeling of self's satisfaction in the gained knowledge, as acquired through that sojourn, ever projects itself in the inner consciousness.

In the one before this we find in the Egyptian forces, when the division in the kingdom came, on account of the rule in the Priesthood. [time of Ra Ta] The entity then in the household of that ruler, and was a favorite with the then ruler, and siding with the ruler, [341] and becoming the chief in that court after the banishment of Priest and those associated, or followers of same. Then first in the name of Isisush. Changed, when the coming of high estate in the rule, to Ahahs, and the entity both developed and retarded in that rule, gaining much of those innate desires toward that of close work with the needle, or with the hand, in any fancy work, for many of the alba garments were then first given shape by those hands, and many may yet be found in those tombs as exist to this day.

As to that which the entity may develop in the present sphere, keep in that same way as has been set in self, in purpose and in manner, for through thy own efforts in self there need not be the necessity in returning to earth's plane [GD's note: She wrote that she considers this earthly life to be a "vale of tears."], for as is set, and if kept, these would develop into the higher spiritual realms, and then keep self in that way that leads to life ever-lasting, for in Him whom thou hast put thy trust is Life, for He is the Way, the Truth, the Light. In Him there is no guile.

We are through for the present.

3. Case #1143
In this next life reading, Cayce frees the soul of [1143] from future challenges in the earth with these words: "*This entity* may, with the keeping of those developments, make its peace in such a manner as for there to be few or none of the turmoils of the earth in its experience again."

Text of Reading 1143-2 F 48
(Secretary, Christian Background)

This Psychic Reading given by Edgar Cayce at the David E. Kahn home, 44 W. 77th St., Apt. 14-W, New York City, this 18th day of April, 1936, in accordance with request made by the self—Miss [1143], Associate Member of the Ass'n for Research & Enlightenment, Inc.

PRESENT

Edgar Cayce; Gertrude Cayce, Conductor; Gladys Davis, Steno. [1143].

READING

Born July 12, 1887, in Leanninghen Spa, England.

Time of Reading London, S.W.I., 11:25 to 12:15 A.M. Eastern Standard Time, England.

(Life Reading Suggestion)

EC: (In going back over years to birth date—"—'26, '25, '24—Changes!— '23, '22—'16—What a change!—'15, '14—" etc., on back to birth date)

Yes, we have the records here as made through the experiences and consciousness of the entity in those spheres of activity that have dealt and do deal with the application of the self and its soul-influences in the present.

As we find from the records here, those periods in the interim between the sojourns of the entity in the earth may be reckoned or paralleled with experiences of the entity in environs about the earth—termed as an astrological influence.

These, however, are mere indications, and as to what an entity does about that the entity sets or maintains as its ideal makes for or produces or brings into the experience of the entity either developments or retardments.

As to the experiences then of this entity, [1143] called in the present (What a beautiful surrounding in its entrance into this earth in the present!), we find in the astrological aspects much has been gained and maintained by the entity that would be well for others to make a part of themselves in their own application.

For while throughout the experiences and sojourns in the earth turmoils of many natures have arisen, especially upon large scales of antagonistic influence, troublesome periods by animosities and waywardnesses upon the part of individuals and groups and masses about the entity, with these the entity has kept an equal balance, especially in what may be termed in words as tolerance.

Not that there have not been anxieties even in its spiritual or astrological aspects, yet these as an innate and as a manifested experience become a portion of the entity itself.

And—as is the fruit of same—patience, as engendered by mercy, has accompanied these experiences.

Thus the phases of the entity's sojourns then in the environs called astrological become apparent as with new meanings to some from those environments.

Jupiter—we find the association as towards a *helpfulness* in the engendering associations with those in power, those in positions of prominence as to their engendering for others conditions that make for the developments towards brotherly love in their activity.

These then make from the material aspect for that upon which the entity is active, finding in its associations great abilities, those that have been entrusted with means, manners and ways of dealing with their fellow man.

And the entity has been, and will ever be so long as these are held, inviolate as a tempering experience for all such.

Also in those influences from Venus we find that beauty, peace, harmonious forces are ever in and *about* the entity; yet for such to become active in the experience there has been required upon the part of the entity an *activity*. Not placidness, but peace rather gained, rather felt, rather experienced by *bringing* same into the experience of others.

We find also in those astrological sojourns or influences in Uranus making for extremes; that the entity through its earthly as well as through the innate forces that have been impelled or chosen by self has found itself swinging, as it were, oft *suddenly* from extreme to extreme.

Yet in its ability from a soul force, that finds expressions in those words we term as tolerance, patience, the entity has found the abilities to aid here and there.

Hold fast to these. For while those influences from the Martian experiences make for turmoils as about, we find that—unless it allows itself to become, as it were, at times sorry for itself, or to become in a manner affected through such experiences that arise for self-aggrandizement—the entity may continue then to bring harmonious influences in the experiences of those whom the entity may contact in the materiality.

These influences, of course, as indicated, arise innately; yet *so well*, so oft have these been manifested in the physical and material application of the entity. To differentiate becomes rather hard in making for an interpretation of that which has been recorded here.

This entity may, with the keeping of those developments, make its peace in such a manner as for there to be few or none of the turmoils of the earth in its experience again.

As to the influences from the sojourns in the earth; while these are not *all*, they are those that in the present make for the urges that the entity finds indicated in its experiences and in its meeting with its fellow man in their problems, in their turmoils.

For, as the entity has in the most of its sojourns from the earth *given—given—given* of self, so has there come in the deeper recesses of the present experience—even upon the heels of turmoils, even upon the mount of consternation—a deeper and an abiding peace that comes only with that as He hath given, "*My peace I leave with you.*" Not as the world knoweth or giveth peace, but that which makes for those answers as from within, when there is the turning to that Great Giver of love, mercy, justice—"Well done, thou good and faithful servant." For ye shall indeed know the joys of thy Lord. Hold fast, stand steadfast with the armor of thy Lord near thee.

Before this we find the entity lived in the earth during those periods when there was the overrunning, or when the changes were coming about in the land of nativity, when there were the Norsemen with the Huns and the Gauls that made for the turmoils in the north and in the eastern portion of the land.

The entity then was in the name (hence it is well name in the present) Marjoriee.

In the experience there were those turmoils and strifes, with neighbor against neighbor oft; for it was during those periods when they each of the landholders or of the different groups were as a law in their own land.

The entity kept a balance between many of those in and about that land, in Lancastershire, where there is to the entity—in those surroundings in the present—much that makes for deep meditation; for sorrow, yet punctured much and oft with a deeper gladness for the experiences that come there.

And as the entity was in those fields and among those blossoms when they began to fade, it finds those sadnesses and yet bring a joy and a comfort in the inner self.

Hence in the introspection of self gladness is ever present, yet it is tinged with the desire for help to those that are weary of their mental and material burdens—that finds an answering within the inmost being of the entity itself.

For as the entity gained in those experiences, so may it in the present find that—not by might nor by power, as saith the Lord of hosts, but by the still small voice, by the counsel as one tempered with mercy, grace and peace—it may bring to those whom the entity contacts in such disturbing forces the experiences of *harmony* within self.

Before that we find the entity was in those periods when there was the return of a chosen people to their land for the reestablishing in the land of promise of a ritual service.

There the entity, with Zerubbabel's handmaids, became a helpful influence. And with the coming then of the priest—or princess—and the prince in Nehemiah, we find the entity lent that aid which made for the helping of those that resisted the peoples roundabout. Not by might, not by power, but by lending a helping hand to those that suffered bodily; aiding in bringing to those a better understanding of that edict which was given by the king for the reestablishing of those services of a peoples in their *own* land.

Then the name was Belenda, and the entity gained, lost, gained through the experience. For being misjudged for the associations with those then as of the heathens roundabout, as termed by those strangers in their own home land, the entity felt within self as being misunderstood—and condemned, when innately within self there was known how the protection was brought even to many of those that labored upon the wall, as well as in those that were established.

Yet if the entity will read very closely the 6th and 8th chapters of Nehemiah, it will find much that harkens for an awareness of its presence there.

Hold to those things that make for this ability to be tolerant, even with those that despitefully use thee. For it engenders strife to hold animosities.

Before that we find the entity was in the land now known as the Egyptian, during those periods when there were turmoils and strifes to those peoples that had settled in the land, and attempted to build for those peoples roundabout an understanding of the relationships of man to the Creative Forces, of man to his own fellow man.

The entity was among those peoples joined nigh to that one made the Priest, and who was debarred or set adrift from the activities begun.

Those periods and experiences brought turmoils to the entity, yet with the return of the Priest, with the activities of those that came from Atlantis, with the paralleling of the teachings by the emissaries from Saneid, from On (?), from the activities in the Gobi, the entity began then to know that he that smiteth thee, if thou dost smite in return, will but engender an animosity that grows, that becomes as briers and tares in thine own experience, that will hinder thee in thine *own* activity, bringing disturbing forces that make for the engendering of hate.

The name then was Absi–Shupht, and much might be said as to that development there.

As to the abilities in the present, and that to which the entity may attain, and how:

Who would dare give the entity counsel when it may counsel so well! Hold fast to that which has been or may be gained by the reading of the 30th chapter of Deuteronomy, the 14th of Joshua, the 24th Psalm, the 12th of Romans; the 14th, 15th, 16th, 17th as recorded to John. For there ye will see that thou hast *innately* made as thy bond. For He *is* in His holy temple and would speak with thee; for *thy* body, *too*, is His temple, and there He meets with thee!

Love the Lord, eschew evil, keep the faith. For it *is* but a reasonable service.

Ready for questions.

Q: *Where can I find this man whom you suggest I should gain further development and training from?*

A: The *more* will be found within self through the study, the application in the daily life of those tenets as recorded in those words that have been given.

Rather than in any man, in any person. For thy development is such, thy purposes are so high, that thou mayest meet Him, find Him, within— through the meditation with thy Lord.

Q: *Do you consider that I have healing ability, and if I used it more would I develop?*

A: The ways are shown as in those references given, that as has been given, "What ye ask, that will be done *in* and through you." Thus not only by the touch but by the meditation, by the handling of bodies, thou mayest—as it were—*quicken* them to their *own* abilities; that the grudges, animosities must be put away.

For the mind is the builder, the spirit is willing; the body should be an expression of these.

Q: Do you consider that I should be a communicant or not?

A: Such answers, to be sure, should come from within. For the church, that of the faith—He is thy bridegroom—the *church* is within thee, the temple is within *thee! There* He meets thee!

If thy service to thy fellow man leads thee to commune, to break the bread, to break the body with others—*He* will guide, *He* will direct.

We are through for the present.

4. Case #560
Editor's Note: In this next case, Cayce identifies this entity's readiness to move beyond earth life: "The earth need hold no cares for the entity in or after this experience."

Text of Reading 560-1 F 45
(Protestant)

This psychic reading given by Edgar Cayce at his office, 105th Street & Ocean, Virginia Beach, Va., this 30th day of September, 1931, in accordance with request made by self—Miss [560].

PRESENT

Edgar Cayce; Gertrude Cayce, Conductor; Gladys Davis, Steno. Misses [560] and [993], Mildred Davis and L. B. Cayce.

READING

Born April 7, 1886, in Hull, England.

Time of Reading 3:00 P.M. Eastern Standard Time. . . . , Virginia.

(Life Reading Suggestion)

EC: Yes, we have the entity and those relations with the universe and universal forces, as are latent and manifested in the entity now known as, or called, [560].

In entering, we find in astrological aspects many *varying* conditions; while Pisces, just past, in the rising of influences from this—with the Mercurian, Venus, Jupiter and Uranus, these bring in an *astrological* manner many *varying* aspects or experiences ⁂ the influence, or the entity influenced in many varying manners as to that as is builded, or has been builded in the present experience of the entity, has depended upon the manner in which the entity itself has applied its will as respecting same. These, as we find, are builded in the entity *for* experiences, *irrespective* of how will's influence *has* been applied. *These*, as we find, have been builded as *how* the entity *has* applied will as respecting same:

In those influences in Mercury—oft has the entity been considered not only high-minded, but tendency towards the dictatorial in mien and manner, though the application of *will* in *respect* to such has altered this in a great degree as to the *influences* impelled by the positiveness *of* the entity in its application toward such influences. *Well* (this aside, please) were the fact, as has been builded by the entity, that many would do likewise.

In the influences in Venus makes for that of one that is loved by all who come to know the entity *as* a whole, yet the application of self respecting same has not *drawn* all to express themselves in a manner as would signify that [in] their feelings toward the entity. Not that the entity had, or has, held self *aloof* from peoples, but rather that, those that have *known* the entity best have learned to love the entity the more. In this application, this has drawn *to* the entity, *for* the entity, friendships that once made *seldom* have they been broken, save by those who have so acted, so acted in their *own* feelings, as to separate themselves from that influence. This has the tendency at times (as the entity has changed much) for the grudges, or the holding of activities of others in a manner—*not* as grudge, but a tendency to not easily forget slights or differences; yet in the *building* much has been lost in the bigness of the influences gained in Jupiter *and* Uranus in this respect, for the *spiritual* life *of* the entity is such as to have *builded* for a development in this *present* plane to such an extent—that is, the *desire* such, and kept in the present attunement—the earth need hold no cares for the entity in or after this experience.

In Jupiter we find one that has broad vision of any subject, no matter how very centralized a portion of the subject or matter is taken by the entity, no matter how definite the aims of the entity towards conditions, peoples, places or *philosophies*—even—the *vision* is that that *enables* the entity to reach far beyond that as is ordinarily understood. With the ascendancy of this influence, after the fifteenth of the coming month, for years there will *still* be the tendency for an expansion of influences in these directions, of enabling others to so centralize their efforts and their visions as to gain a better concept of that portion of life's experience they, or individuals, are seeking. Hence, as one that would direct in the centralizing of individuals' desires for the seeking of spiritual guidance, mental understanding, material aid in a physical sphere, will *be* the work, the greater developing period of, and *abilities* of the entity in this present experience.

In those influences in Uranian, makes for those little appearances of indifference in the entity's mien, when it has as much curiosity as any! yet the appearance and acts may be as not the interest, but desiring not to show to be curious, or to delve into other peoples' affairs or business! yet the influences as are seen, that oft the entity—in its *intuitive* natures— if asked, could often help when others *feel* indifference has kept them from seeking when they would desire to. This, in the application, the entity has kept rather as a sacred portion of its own experience. At times it has brought those qualms of conscience that has made for wonderments as to whether it has appeared too indifferent or not, or as to whether there has been as much interest shown as self *should* have manifested or expressed; yet with the opportunities as may be opened through those experiences with the rising influence in Jupiter—which will bring, with the square of Venus in the love's influence, as is seen, many experiences that will make for a larger, fuller, greater understanding to the entity in these coming years, and months, and days.

In the appearances, then, and their *influence* in the present experience:

In the one then just before this we find in the land chosen *now* as the dwelling land [Virginia], and among those peoples as settled in the new

land. The entity's experiences were of those that were *leading* as fron-
tiersmen, yet in a period when those of the earth had brought forth
those of bounty to the people, yet during the period of oppression, and
during those periods as brought on by the aggressiveness of those sires
in the period of the entity in the Fairfax land. The entity lost through
those oppressions, and losing the life early in the experience by being
crushed in earth; and masses brings that *physical* innate influence of
crowds, or *smothering feelings* close to the entity, as if it must *soon* be free!
In this experience the entity finds that while there are *many* who boast
of their lineage, or of their relations, rather does *self* find that, that *builded*
as to aiding another speaks much more than that as of OTHERS' accomplishments for them. *proud* indeed of the associations and relations,
as all should be—for to have *chosen* a way that brings its reward in the
material way may one be proud, yet not haughty *with* same. In this experience gaining and losing. Losing under the expressions of those that
would oppress, yet *gaining* in the love held even for those that oppressed.

In the one then before this we find in that land of nativity (that is, of
the present) [England], during those periods when there were those rebellions *through* the land, and the entity of those in the household of
him, the ruler, that was beheaded [Charles I]. The entity then gained
through the oppressions in that land, being able then to aid those that
were *of* that house, even she [Queen Henrietta] that suffered by the acts
of those that took the life *of* the ruler. The entity aided in making for the
quietings of the fears, through those teachings of the faith that makes
one strong, even under physical oppression. Being also among those
that gave aid to the young king [Charles II] in his escape to the foreign
land, aiding also with those that cared for this ruler in the foreign land,
becoming an emissary—or what would be called in the present a political spy, the entity was able to give much aid in *material* ways, and with
the spiritual guidance as held, much of a mental and *spiritual* aid to
those contacted. In the name Erial. In the present experience, while
those experiences of the period bring many of those little hesitancies as
come from speaking when there is the thought of things to be done or
accomplished, yet gives to the entity the insight of a broad field of experience.

In the one before this we find in that land now known as the promised land, and during that period when there were the walkings in the land of the Promised One. The entity among those that were close *to* the Master, being then the sister to one of those that the Master raised from the dead [Lazarus] living in Bethany in that experience. Hence those of that period are near and dear, and far *from* those things that hinder from *knowing* of those that would separate the entity from those experiences! Gaining, sure, through the experience, and giving much to many; though called by those that in the experience would bring censure for the parts chosen [as Martha], or those of the secular things of life, yet in the present—with the experience—brings that *practicability* of the entity, that in groups, in associations, has ever been called—while the dreamer, yet all *practical* thought must be in accord *with* the life lived, with the circumstances as surround, with the conditions in which people find themselves—*these* are the better part, as was in that experience.

In the one then before this we find in that land when there were those comings together in the land now known as the Persian or Arabian land, when Uhjltd gathered many peoples about those cities being builded. The entity among those that came in, and were of those that—in the *household* of the leader—came in contact with, associated *with*, many of those of the household. In this association the entity changed much in its attitude towards people, things, conditions and surroundings. Hence in this experience may be termed the change in the entity's activities, as is seen what was brought in the one that followed. In this experience may be seen that as has been builded, or as has been overcome, of the little grudges, or the little feelings oft of slight or of oppressions, "I will get even at sometime—not *mine*, but it will be done!" This may be overcome, *has* been overcome much, may it be taken away—even as has been given. In this experience in the name Raoue.

In the one then before this we find in that land now known as the Egyptian, and during that period when there were rebellions in the land, and when there had been the reestablishing of those that were deposed. The entity came into the *temple* service there, being *then* closely associated with the priest as was deposed [Ra Ta], and became close to those that were of the temple service, gaining in the experience, losing only when the secular things of the world—when the entity sent abroad with others—made forgetfulness come in the experience of the entity in that period. In the name Isusi. In the present, this experience has—as of those in desert and in the Holy City—brought much of that, with the Uranian influence, that makes for abilities to aid in an understanding of that as *is* the *desire* of those that would seek. Being practical, there makes for those abilities—as to whether that sought is of the *material* sources, the spiritual foundations, or of a mental aptitude towards the attempts to cover up or hide the real purpose. In this field, then, may the entity gain the most in the present, in aiding those who would seek to find— in the various forces as they manifest in the entity's experience—*that* which *that* individual seeks. That is, as the entity—through its breadth of experience and understanding—may aid another in knowing what phase *of* the forces *manifested* an individual may find *their* greater bless- ing.

In the present, then, keep—as was in old—those experiences that make for the *understanding* of those forces *in* love as were manifested in the home in Bethany. Keep that committed, for those that seek *through* love will find. Those that seek through any *other* source may be dumb- founded in the maze of that as is presented. Ready for questions.

Q: *Would it be advisable for the body to change her name to that of Mildred instead of Mary as it now is? [GD's note: It is interesting to observe that Miss [295], who was told that she was "Mary of Bethany," subsequently changed her middle name from "Gertrude" to "Mary."]*

A: Those vibrations as come with the changes in the astrological ex- perience, as well as the numerological experiences, would be well for such a change made in the coming or present experience *upon* the en- tity.

Q: *Did the body desire to be born in England, and why?*

A: In those surroundings as were the experiences *of* the entity, as has been seen, *were* those surroundings *of* that particular sphere. Rather *was* the seeking to return *through* those channels to the land where oppres- sions had been, and an awakening had been in the entity's experience. Hence the *opportunity* offered itself *to* be born in England, to reach that as it had desired in its karmic or karma influence in the experience—see?

Q: *What was the name of the entity just before the present one?*

A: Fairfax.

Q: *What was the name in Bethany?*

A: The one, the sister to Mary—Martha.

Q: *In the name as Fairfax, was she related to the one who is her sister in the present [993], who was also a Fairfax?*

A: A sister.

Q: *How may we cooperate in our new work?*

A: This rather indefinite, yet these may be seen. As one has *ever* been a complement to the other, so in the *activities* will there be *kept* that same position in the activities of those as are approached.

Q: *Why has the entity so much fear in the present?*

A: The experiences of the entity through the various appearances has brought those of fear in *many*, as is seen. In the present then, there will be seen, as through that which brought fear in a *physical* sense, will be eradicated through the awakening in the spiritual application *of* material, as well as physical activities. See?

Q: *What was the entity's first name as a Fairfax?*

A: Geraldine.

Q: *Are there any records in the present available on this?*

A: There are some—these may be found even in stone.

Q: *What was the father's name, as Fairfax?*

A: This will be found among those of the records in that land about the Fredericksburg, where these were, you see.

We are through for the present.

5. Case #2903

Editors Note: In this next case, Cayce identifies this soul as "one who may, with the present will forces, make self unnecessary for return in earth's spheres."

Text of Reading 2903-1 M 58
(Life Insurance, Special Representative)

This psychic reading given by Edgar Cayce at his office, 322 Grafton Avenue, Dayton, Ohio, this 26th day of June, 1925, in accordance with request made by self—Mr. [2903].

PRESENT

Edgar Cayce; Mrs. Cayce, Conductor; Gladys Davis, Steno.

Mrs. [265], sister of [2903].

READING

Born January 2, 1867, near Hopkinsville, Ky.

Time of Reading 4:00 P.M. Dayton Savings Time. . . . , Tenn.

GC: You will give the relation of this entity and the Universe, and the Universal Forces, giving the conditions that are as personalities, latent and exhibited, in the present life. Also the former appearances in the earth's plane, giving time, place, and the name, and that in that life which built or retarded the development for the entity, giving the abilities of the present entity and to that which it may attain, and how.

EC: Yes, we have the entity here, and those relations with the Universal Forces as are latent and exhibited in the present earth's plane. There come many of the conditions coming as urges from the existences in the earth's plane, and those surrounding influences, as are shown, have been manifested and may be manifested in the earth's plane.

As to the present position, we find taken from that of Jupiter, with Mercury and Mars in both adverse and in good influences in the present earth's plane. Then, we find one with those high ennobling influences as come from both Jupiter and Mercury's influence. Then one of high ennobling life and manner of manifesting same in the earth's plane. One with a high temper, yet able of controlling same and turning same into those channels wherein the better influence comes to self and others.

One, then, that gives much more to the development of others in every plane. One that has little of the influences towards detrimental conditions toward the development in the plane.

One who may, with the present will forces, make self unnecessary for return in earth's spheres.

One who, with the ennobling influences in Jupiter, brings much of this world's goods to the use of self and of others in whom there may come the influence as is seen in the mental forces.

In the development then in those of adverse forces, we find one in whom many of the influence of wrath and of that of the excess of the desire to hinder has at times brought consternation to the individual, yet each has been turned into that of development of self and beneficial to those whom the entity contacts.

One, then, of a loving, noble, influence in lives of all whom the entity contacts. One that causes others to have faith, confidence, in self and in others. One that invites, through the radiations of unselfishness in self, the desire of others and in others to give more of their self in the earth's plane towards development.

One that finds the greater possibilities in self to give aid in every manner to others. One who would have made a *wonderful* minister in the present earth's plane. One who would have made success in ministration, or any of the developments of either economic or political forces. One that may yet in the branch of the influence towards those who labor in that of service to others, this entity may guide and direct many. This, and the usage of same, we will find in the urges from appearances.

In the appearances then:

In the one before this, we find in that of him who gave the freedom to the peoples in the English rule, when the peoples rose and sought freedom from the yoke of the King. Then in the name, Oliver Cromwell, and the entity then fought for that principle in which there was then instilled in the inmost forces, and in the present we find that urge for the ability of each individual to find their place and to fill same in their best capacity, and in this also we find that desire ever is shown in the entity to give of the best, and not reserving self in any manner.

In the one before this, we find in the days of the wars in the Grecian forces. The entity then in that of him who led the forces in the raids in the Western portion of the country. Also leading the peoples to the higher understanding of self, and seeking to educate them in that which would give the better influence in their homes. Then in the name Xenophon, and in this we find in the present the urge and ability to so direct the lives of others that the best may come to them. The detrimental forces coming from these being that of the warriors in the flesh, being fearful of same.

In the one before this, we find in the Egyptian forces; when the second rule that gave the peoples the laws as pertaining to the worship, the entity then in the Counselor to the then ruler, and in the name of Cenraden, and was that one who assisted, especially, in the memorials as were set and placed in the land during that day, being then in the manner the historian and gatherer of data for those of that period. The present urge we find, especially, in that in the desire to know, especially, of these periods, as the entity has and will show, passed through in the earth and in other planes. The entity developed again in this.

In the one before this, we find in the now Peruvian country, when the peoples were destroyed in the submerging of the land. The entity then in that of the next to the ruler in the Ohlm [Ohm?—Ohum? Aymara?] rule, and in the name of Ormdi, and the entity then gave much to the peoples, especially to those who furnished the building of the lands for the sustenance of the peoples. In that, we find the present urge from same comes to the entity through the desire to understand the position from which any group of peoples desire their cause presented to others.

As to the abilities and how to develop same in the present, we find the entity may give much counsel to those whom would serve others, and in that capacity the entity will find the greatest development for self, and the ability to do same will and is presented to the entity from time to time.

Many days will be seen in the present earth's plane. Then keep in that way wherein Him who gives the good and perfect gifts may be made manifest before men, knowing that unto Him all honor is due.

6. Case #2112

Editor's Note: Cayce states this entity's freedom clearly: "The entity has set self aright. As to what it may attain lies only with self, for kept—and keeping the faith—never would it be necessary for the entity to enter again into *this* vale, but rather to bask or journey through that presence of the faithful!"

Text of Reading 2112-1 F 58
(Apt. House Manager, Theosophist)

This psychic reading given by Edgar Cayce at his office, 115 West 35th Street, Virginia Beach, Va., this 2nd day of June, 1931, in accordance with request made by self—Mrs. [2112].

PRESENT

Edgar Cayce; Gertrude Cayce, Conductor; Gladys Davis, Steno. Mrs. [2112] and Mrs. Walker.

READING

Born April 29, 1873, in Norfolk, Va.

Time of Reading 3:30 P.M. Eastern Standard Time. . . . , Va.

(Life Reading Suggestion)

EC: Yes, we have the entity and those relations with the universe and universal forces.

In entering we find the astrological influences of the entity, [2112], are quite different from that as has been *builded* in the entity in the present; for while there has been three stages of development in the present experience, those in the last three to four *years* has changed so that things that do appear in the present are but the shadow of that as would be seen from an astrological influence; for the entity has applied the will's influence in such a manner in the present—especially the latter portion of the present experience—in such a manner as to have made a *wonderful* development.

In giving, then, astrological and that builded, these must be seen can *only* be relative, and—as there has been an alteration—these must not be *confused* with developments, or with the will's influence altering the *astrological* aspect.

Coming under the influence of Mercury with Venus, naturally makes for a mental aptitude for the entity, but the quieting effect that the entity has upon individuals that the entity contacts is *builded* by the will's influence upon that as has become a portion *of* the entity's experience, even though the experience in Venus gives that love for peace, understanding, contentment, hope, faith, vision, longsuffering, endurance, loving-kindness, and those of *brotherly* love; for these being *grounded* in that as has been experienced by the entity, the *hope* as is *manifest* in the present comes from that communion with the higher sources themselves; for he that seeks shall find, and he that knocketh to him shall be opened. Few have gained the insight into what *this* means as the entity has! Be *not* overcome with the long waiting, nor be not *weary* in well-doing; for the *Master* learned obedience, even through the things which *He* suffered.

In contemplation, then, of those abilities within self, of those desires of those wanting to aid through the efforts of thine own hands—do well that thou hast in hand from day to day, and there will be given that peace, that joy, that understanding, that only comes from the knowledge of God lives! And His Son is in the world! Through faith in His name may we know and see and understand all that the *physical*, the *mental*, has to bear in this mundane sphere.

In the abilities of the entity, these may only be measured by that ability of the entity to remain in that understanding, that knowledge, as has come *to* the entity in the last few years; for, as each body meets its own problems from day to day with that understanding that the increase, the love, the desires are to be kept open in a manner that is in keeping with His Son, *God* gives the increase. Be not in that position of one that frets about things, conditions, or peoples not *doing as you* would have them do! You may only be the channel through which the reflection of His love may be *made* manifest, for *God* works in His *own* way, own manner, and fretting self only brings those of discouragement, disillusions, as to those things that *He* would bring to pass.

Speak gently, speak kindly to those who falter. Ye know not *their* own temptation, nor the littleness of their understanding. Judge not as to this or that activity of another; rather pray that the light may shine even in *their* lives as it *has* in thine. These are the manners in which the sons and daughters of men may *know* His way. In this mundane sphere there comes to all that period when doubts and fears arise, even to doubting thine *own* self. These may *easily* be cast aside by knowing that He is *in* His holy temple and *all* is well.

In the conditions that come from those things that are in the past, let the dead bury their *own* dead; for *He* is God of the living, *not* of the dead! He is Life, and Light, and Immortality! *Glory* in His weakness, *glory* in His might, *glory* in His watchful-loving-kindness, and *all will* be right!

In the appearances and the effect these have, *have had*, upon the present experience:

In the one before this we find in that land now known as the Eastern or New England land, where those persecutions came for those who had the visions of the familiar spirits, or for those who saw those that walked in the shadow land. The entity was then among those who were of the household of one who suffered in body for the *persecutions* as were brought to the household. In the name Mary Alden. The entity gained and lost through this experience, for when persecutions came, hardships came upon the entity and there were grudges held against those who brought bodily suffering to the loved ones of the entity. In the present there has ever been innate an awe to the entity of those who were teachers, ministers, preachers, or those who professed *any* association with unseen sources, and a dread to know the *end* of such! Also this has brought about much of that that has changed the entity *in* understanding as to following what has been *ordinarily* termed orthodox forces, or religious beliefs.

In the one before this we find in that land, that period, when there were contentions, wars and rumors of wars in those lands that were overrun by the peoples who—zealous of their beliefs—came into the land to conquer it. The entity was then among those in the household of that called the Moslems, and while the entity held to those tenets of the fathers in the experience, yet the entity offered much aid and succor to those who became—as they were—the *prisoners* of that people. The entity then was in the name Telulila. In this experience the entity *gained* throughout, holding to that as taught put into practice that as had been gained in the inner self through *another* association. In the contact with individuals the entity gave that as was *inmost* in self as truth. In the present has come those influences ever that has held the entity to those of a high ideal as to moral, material, and spiritual laws.

In the one before this we find in that land now called the Holy Land, and about that land where the Master walked—the entity then a sister of she whom the entity met at the well in the land, and the entity came to know of that ministry, following afar; yet later becoming one of those that *spread* those glad tidings to those in Mount Seir. In the name Selmaa. In this experience the entity lost and gained. Lost in the early portion when there was the aggrandizing of selfish interests; gaining in crucifying of *ideas* for ideals, and gained much through the latter portion of that experience. In the present there is felt that awe that comes with the hearing of that particular portion of the Scripture, the Gospel, the Message read, of the journey *through* that land; and the *abilities* with the needle, with the making of things that have to do with adorning of body, also come from this experience.

In the one before this we find in that land now called the Egyptian, and during that period when there were divisions in the land through the exiling of priest, through the gathering of those that made war through the divisions as were brought. The entity was then among those in the temple during the exile, remaining there, also aiding in the upbuilding when there was the return and the re-establishing. The entity was then the priestess to the Inner Shrine, making self of no estate that the *idea* as held respecting the *ideal* set by same might be kept intact. Losing in respect from many; gaining in self's own abilities to build that toward that which is set as *right*; being hardheaded, as some would term; being set in ways, as others would call; being graceful, peaceful, lovable and law abiding, as others would term. In the name Al-Lai, and there *still* may be seen in the holy mount—or that tomb yet not uncovered—much of that the entity made as respecting the hangings, the accoutrements for the altar in the temple of that day. In the present, that innate feeling of a certain rote, routine, and the entity is—as may ever be seen with self, with household, with others—keeping in a direct line.

In the abilities of the entity in the present, and that to which it may attain:

As has been given, the entity has set self aright. As to what it may attain lies only with self, for kept—and keeping the faith—never would it be necessary for the entity to enter again into *this* vale, but rather to bask or journey through that presence of the faithful!

Ready for questions.

Q: Would it be best for me to take over the house next to my present home, which I have been contemplating?

A: Would be well.

Q: Will the financial part of my present home be worked out satisfactorily?

A: As we find, it will be worked out satisfactorily. Some disappointing factors arising in same, yet will be made satisfactory.

Q: Have I any healing power?

A: What power *hasn't* the body, with that faith, with that *understanding*! These may be used in *many* directions by the laying on of hands, and with prayer—anointing as of oil—as has been given, anointing with oil—pouring in of those of the spirit, that knowledge, of understanding—will bring *blessings* to many. Do not *neglect* that that has been committed into thy keeping—thine own!

Q: *Is the application I use sufficient, or could the phenomena give a better one?*

A: That as may be gained by self the better, than that that may be told; for why take it from another source when self may attain to the Throne itself! *We* are through.

7. Case #444

Editor's Note: This next entity has reached a level of freedom that the decision to reincarnate is hers to make: "Only through the desire may it be necessary for the entity to enter earth's environs again."

Text of Reading 444-1 F 43
(Artist, M.D., Psychiatrist, Educator)

This psychic reading given by Edgar Cayce at Lillian Edgerton, Inc., 267 Fifth Avenue, New York City, this 16th day of November, 1933, in accordance with request made by self—Miss [444], new Associate Member of the Ass'n for Research & Enlightenment, Inc., recommended by Dr. [961].

PRESENT

Edgar Cayce; Hugh Lynn Cayce, Conductor; Gladys Davis, Steno. [444] and [445].

READING

Born May 14, 1890, in New York City.

Time of Reading 11:05 to 11:40 A.M. Eastern Standard Time. New York City.

(Life Reading Suggestion)

EC: Yes, we have the entity and those relations with the universe and universal forces, that are latent and manifested in the personality of the entity now known as [444].

In giving that which may be helpful to the entity in the present, the approach to the astrological influences would be from the sojourns rather than the position of the planets or the elements in same. For, the sojourns make for innate influences; while the earth's appearances make for the greater urge within the present mental forces of the entity.

In this entity, [444], we find rather unusual developments in the astrological influences; for these are rather as *two* urges in the inner being of the entity, or are rather in pairs. So, there will be seen in the present experience that there are periods when there have often been halting opinions or urges leading in separate directions at or during the same period of activity in the physical experience of the entity.

We find that Venus with Uranus make for rather at times the complications as to the character of associations, the activities in the relationships to those influences which are accredited to the activities of an indwelling in such environ. Hence the mystic, the occult, with love's influence, are of particular interest. Hence the entity's abilities in building or making or writing stories pertaining to activities in these directions might be developed in those periods particularly when there is the conjunction of, or the influence direct in the earth from Venus and Uranus experience.

In the activity also in Jupiter do we find the entity's indwelling, making for innate urges in the activity of the entity through those influences that make for travel, for meeting of individuals in the varied walks of life, in those that find expressions in the activity with the mental proclivities of the individual. Rather does the entity innately deal with mental and mind than with things, yet conditions as produced by the mental association and activity of individuals are of particular interest to the entity.

As to the sojourns in the earth and their influence upon the activities of the entity in the present:

Before this we find the entity was during those periods in the present land of nativity when there was an expression of those influences in the spiritualistic realm, in and about those places in Salem, when there were the students and the persecution of those that made for activities in that particular experience.

During the sojourn the entity gained much by the physical activities in following much that was presented in the appearance of those particular phenomena manifested by those felt by many during the period as being possessed.

The entity was rather the observer than associating self with the activities during the period, and was in the name Beldon.

From that experience in the present sojourn there are seen in the activities of the entity those things pertaining to following the lines of suggestions in those activities in that particular experience. And the *mental* forces of those that are active in such fields make for the greater expression of manifestation to the entity.

The fields of reading, the fields of activity in the social relationships, arise from experiences in that sojourn.

Before this we find the entity was during that period when there were the activities of those that came into the land of promise as Crusaders for a cause, in the ideas of many.

The entity then was of the people in the Fatherland, as may be called, that were among those left by the other members of the household; and much of the duties and activities in material things fell upon the shoulders or activities of the entity in the experience, bringing to the entity many questions as to duty and obligation to those influences in the actual experience and duties and obligations that arise from impelling influences or urges to become active in or for an ideal.

Through the experience the entity may be said to have lost and gained, for there was much turmoil in the mental forces of the entity during the period, much of those experiences that made for the realizing of the necessities of material activities in a material world. Yet, in the later portion, as in those experiences when self lost self—as it were—in that it gave to others, in the character of conditions that made for the losing of self in service to others, developments came to the entity. The name then was Herzenderf.

The entity in the experience made for those activities that in the present at times have caused the *wondering* as to the abilities of differentiation—in the experience of self—between that of practical value in the experiences of man or of self and that having more to do with the urge to the emotional influences that make for the forming of ideas, rather than ideals; or as to whether the ideals are of such standards that both the emotional and the practical influence on material things weigh well in the balance of the activities of the individuals through which the relationships bring those influences in their lives and their experience.

Hence the entity naturally in the present is of an analytical mind, with the abilities to use or apply self in analyzing others' influences or experiences in such a way as to be beneficial to such individuals who make overtures to the entity in any manner for aid in this direction. And *well* may the entity apply this experience, for not only self-development but in giving out to others those things that maybe most helpful in their experience. For, the entity learned in that experience, in that land, it is not what a mind *knows* but what the mind applies or does about that it knows, that makes for soul, mental or material advancements.

Before this we find the entity was in that land now known as the Egyptian, during those experiences when there were turmoils and strifes through the rebellions that arose in those activities in that land, when there had been the banishment of the priest in the spiritual life—and the uprisings of the natives and those people that had sojourned in the land, and the differentiations that arose from those tenets that were being proclaimed by those incoming from the Atlantean land.

The entity then was among those that aided in re-establishing the priest among the peoples, and was of those that aided specifically in the Temples of Sacrifice of that period. Not where offerings were made of animals or of the influence or increasing of the field, but where rather those things were shifted from individuals' experience, mentally and materially, that prevented their becoming more in accord with the laws that were proclaimed by the priest—aided and abetted by the activities of those that came in from the Atlantean land to establish what was in the period the greater understanding of the law of the relationships of souls to the Creative Forces, and of the individual's obligations and relations to the fellow man.

Throughout the experience the entity developed in soul, and met many of those that were antagonistic to the influencing for the betterment and many of those through whom the tenets came for the activities in giving and spreading to the peoples that which was helpful in their relationships, their experiences. The entity was particularly active in the later portion, given to disseminating those that were of the fields of activity in what became or is the basis of much in modern medicine.

Before this we find the entity was in those experiences in the Atlantean land, before those periods of the second upheavals or before the lands were divided into the isles.

The entity was among those of the household of the leaders of the One, and made for and aided in the attempts to establish for those that were developing or incoming from the thought forces into physical manifestations to gain the concept of what their activities should be to develop towards a perfection in physical body, losing many of those appurtenances that made for hindrances for the better activities in the experience. The entity then was in the name Asme, as would be put in the language of the day. And the entity gained and lost in the experience. For, while in the office of the priestess in the temple of the One, the entity lost in the associations of the carnal influences in relationships to those in the same activity. Yet, the entity gained in the greater portion of the abilities to make for disseminating truths to others.

In the present also may come, by turning within, from that experience, that which may make for the background of many of those experiences in the writings or in the stories or in the impressions that may be had as illustrative to those whom the entity would teach.

As to the abilities of the entity and that to which it may attain in the present, and how:

In those fields of activity as indicated, the mental influences are above the normal, or above the rabble. And, if the entity will apply self in those forces that make for the creating within self and those whom the entity may contact day by day, ideals that are of the standards making for Creative influences in the mind, the soul and the physical influences, through same may the entity gain and develop in this experience to those influences where only through the desire may it be necessary for the entity to enter earth's environs again.

Then, present self to those influences that make for Creative activities in such a manner that self may never fear to meet that it has spoken in word, or thought; for each soul meets that it has meted, with those measures with which it has meted out.

Ready for questions.

Q: Does this cover all the incarnations that have been passed through this entity?

A: By no means. These are the ones that influence the most in the present.

Q: *What was the name in the Egyptian incarnation?*

A: El-Pthut.

Q: *Give the dates of the Egyptian incarnation.*

A: During that period of the rebellions that were, as would be counted in earth years in the present, 10,490 to 10,300 before the Prince of Peace came into the earth. In the period the entity's activities were such as to make for material development with the associations of the priest Ra Ta, with those of Ra—in the names that came later—and those of that particular period.

Q: *Were there any other periods of incarnation of an Egyptian nature?*

A: During those periods when there were the activities of those just before the return of those peoples from the land to the Promised Land, during the reign of Hathersput [Hatshepsut] [The former was my spelling from the sound. GD]. The entity then was among those peoples. Yet this does not influence the greater portion in the present, as to the mental activities or soul development. Urges may be raised from these, specifically as to things that pertain to the manner in which stones of certain characters are set; for these appear at times—but do not influence the soul development.

Q: *Would you give more details regarding the period of incarnation mentioned in relation with the promised land?*

A: It was during that period when there were the correlations between those of the Princess of the Egyptian and those of the household of one of the tribes of the people there. Then entity was a sister then of Hathersput, the Princess that became the Queen that made for much of the expansions and developments in the land as related to extending the activities of the peoples to other lands. Yet these activities and associations with the people of the period do not influence the soul development as do those that we have given.

We are through for the present.

8. Case #1472

Editor's Note: This case has little need for a return to earth, unless she wishes to help others—the *Bodhisattva* role in Buddhism. Here are

Cayce's words on this: "If there is kept that purpose in self, there is little need for a return; save as one that may lead the way to those that are still in darkness."

Text of Reading 1472-1 F 57
(Writer, Radio Broadcaster, Protestant)

This Psychic Reading given by Edgar Cayce at the David E. Kahn home, 20 Woods Lane, Scarsdale, N.Y., this 6th day of November, 1937, in accordance with request made by the self—Mrs. [1472], new Associate Member of the Ass'n for Research & Enlightenment, Inc., recommended by Mr. [1151] and Mrs. [1158].

PRESENT

Edgar Cayce; Gertrude Cayce, Conductor; Gladys Davis, Steno. Mrs. [1472].

READING

Born May 5, 1880, in Bowling Green, Virginia.

Time of Reading 3:50 to 4:50 P.M. Eastern Standard Time. New York City.

(Life Reading Suggestion)

(In going back over years from present—"—'85—rather as a cross—'84, '83—" etc., on back to birth date.)

EC: Yes, we have the records here of that entity now known as or called [1472].

In giving the interpretations of these, we find these are those that may be helpful in the experience of the entity through the present sojourn.

These are beautiful in many of the experiences, yet the more turmoil may appear to be present in this present sojourn.

For the entity has come a long way, and oft grows weary with the burdens not only that become a part of self's experience but that apparently are unburdened and yet burdened upon the entity, in its dealings with those about self.

Remember, though, that these *are* but that which is a part of the experience; for those whom He loveth, those He holdeth dear in their dealings with the fellow man.

For He hath indeed given His angels charge concerning thee, and He will bear thee up—if ye will faint not but hold to that purpose whereunto thou hast purposed in thy tabernacle in the present.

For know that His temple in thee is *holy*; and thy body-mind is indeed the temple of the living God.

Thus may ye find oft that upon the horns of the altar many of the burdens may be laid aside, and that the sweet incense of faith and hope and prudence and *patience* will arise to bring the consciousness and the awakening of the glories that may be thine.

In giving, for this entity, the interpretations of the records made—upon time and space from God's book of remembrance—we find life, as a whole, is a continuous thing; emanating from power, energy, God-Consciousness, ever.

And as it must ever be, so has it ever been; so that only a small vista or vision may be taken here and there, from the experiences of the entity in those environs of an astrological nature (as ye term).

Or the experiences of the visitation of the soul-entity, as it were, during those periods when absent from the material, three-dimensional matter, become as in the accord with that which has been accredited by the students—yea, by the seers of old to those astrological aspects.

That is, the influences or environs to the entity in those consciousnesses that are given as a portion of the experience, from such sojourns, are as signs or symbols or emblems in the experience of the entity in the present.

For as the entity experiences, it is ever the *now* and what the entity or soul may do *about* the consciousness or awareness that makes for those influences which are to be.

Hence such influences that are accredited much to the astrological aspects become a portion of the entity, not because of the position at the time of birth but because of the entity's sojourn there. Or, rather, because the All-Wise, All-Creative Force has given into the keeping of the souls that they journey as it were from experience or awareness or consciousness to consciousness, that they—as a portion of the whole—

may become aware of same.

And as the injunction has been from the beginning, subdue ye the influences from without, that ye may be a fit companion, that you may be one with that Creative Force or Energy ye worship as thy Maker, thy God, thy Brother—yea, that within which ye live, ye move, ye have your being!

Then as we find, as the consciousness is aware of the individual now, and knows itself to be itself—these are the purposes.

Then only as an individual gives itself in service does it become aware. For as the divine love has manifested, does become manifested, that alone ye have given away do ye possess. That *alone* is the manner in which the growth, the awareness, the consciousness grows to be.

For until the experiences are thine, thy awareness cannot be complete.

As to the astrological aspects, we find these become as innate or mental—or dream, or visions, or cries, or voices as it were from within.

But the influences that arise from the few appearances in the material sojourns or consciousness (that have an effect in the present) are to create or bring about or affect the emotions.

Hence as there are those contacts with individual entities—for this entity is struggling even as they—there comes with the awareness of their thought-expression in material consciousness the emotions, the awareness of their struggles having been as parallel, or at cross purposes here or there.

Yet having left as it were upon the skein of time and space that consciousness that only in the patience of the divine love may that hope, that helpfulness be made complete—as ye lean upon the arm of thy Brother, thy Friend, ye may be borne to the very presence of divinity itself.

In the astrological aspects then we find these as a part of this entity's experience; that Jupiter, Mars, Venus, Uranus, Neptune all become a portion of the entity's innate activity.

Hence these come into material manifestation by the application of, or doing something about, the urge produced by that activity that is latent yet is so subtle, yet so definite as to produce that which brings movement to the experience of self.

Thus it becomes a portion of its activity in the material sojourn.

Venus and Jupiter bring sympathy, love, beauty; and those abilities to depict same into material activity such that it becomes a portion of the longings and the hopes of the many.

For as thoughts are things, and as their currents run into the experience of individuals, they shape lives and activities so that they become miracles or crimes in the experiences of others as they mete them in their associations with their fellow men.

For as ye do it unto the least of these, thy brethren, ye do it unto thy Maker.

Hence these make for those activities in the experience of this entity's soul in which the masses, as well as classes and groups, are to be, will be, influenced.

Hence is there little wonder that oft there is the second thought—yea, the counsel with the inner self—as to whether that written, that spoken, that printed, that said in thy dealings with others becomes as a wonderment or is constructive or destructive?

But more and more may the thoughts expressed and given out by the entity bring constructive activity in the lives of others, as the self gains that open consciousness that He has given His angels charge lest ye dash thy foot against a stone.

Hence know that He is in His holy temple, and that all the earth must hear, must know. For every knee must bow to that love divine, as ye are capable of meting and measuring through such activities in thy experience and thy relationships with thy fellow men.

In Mars we find those fits of anger, resentment, selfishness here and there; those impure motives creating those struggles, those entanglements, those angers. Yet these as they arise upon thy horizon of activity in thy relationships may oft keep from view the visions of that glory prepared for those who love the Lord.

Yet know that truth and light, as may be aroused or made alive from the assurances of His walks with thee, will dissipate those fogs, those mists, as ye apply love in thy dealings with every character of circumstance in thy experience with others.

Then these will matter little; for the Lord's ways are not past finding out, yet ye must oft learn to wait upon the Lord, and not become overanxious—in thy anxiety that "they, too" taste of the goodness that may be found in the divine love.

In Uranus, as well as in Neptune, we find the water—yea, the elementals; the fire and water—oft interfering? no, cleansing rather. For as hath been given, all must be tried so as by fire. All must be purified.

Yet in the beauty of life springing anew in the water of life itself, ye find in the mysteries—yea, the occult and the spiritual forces—influences that make for *extremes* in the lives of many.

Yet as He walked the path to Gethsemane, [Jesus] as He struggled alone with His own Cross; so ye—as ye struggle *have* the assurance that His presence abideth; and they that become overzealous or overanxious may find that the stepping-stones that may be in thy experience become stumbling-stones.

But keep ye the faith in not the Cross as sacrifice but the Cross as the *way*, the *light*, the *life*!

For without the Cross there is not the Crown!

As to the appearances in the earth, all may not be visioned from this particular experience or sojourn. For as ye apply thyself in thy daily experiences in bringing those bonds here, those activities in the sojourns of others, ye bring the *new* visions and vistas of thy sojourns materially as well as in the astrological spheres about this thine own concept of the universe. But:

Before this we find the entity was in the land of the present nativity, during those periods of the settlings in the early portions of the land.

It was when there were those being brought into the land for companions, helpmeets to those of the land.

The entity was among those brought hither from the English land, and become in the household of that family which later grew to be in authority, in power, in that Virginian land; or in the household of that family whose name has been changed to what is now called Byrd—then Bayonne [?].

In the experience, as Clementine, the entity's activities were in the assurance of the freedom of actions for the bringing not only of conveniences into the home but into the activities of the neighboring groups roundabout.

And these have left upon the consciousness of the entity such emotions that oft it finds itself bound by convention, bound by that which prevents the full expression.

Yet know in the awareness that ye will find more and more that the *truth* indeed sets one *free*. *Not* to convention, of the material policies or activities, but in *spirit and in truth!*

For God looks upon the purposes, the ideals of the heart, and not upon that which men call convention.

Before that we find the entity was in the Palestine land, during those days when the Master walked in the earth; and when there were the peoples about those activities of not only the birth but His sojourns before and after the return from Egypt—those whom Judy blessed, that labored in the preserving of the records of *his* activities as the Child; the activities of the Wise Men, the Essenes and the groups to which Judy had been the prophetess, the healer, the writer, the recorder—for all of these groups.

And though questioned or scoffed by the Roman rulers and the tax gatherers, and especially those that made for the levying or the providing for those activities for the taxation, the entity gained throughout.

Though the heart and body was often weary from the toils of the day, and the very imprudence—yea, the very selfishness of others for the aggrandizing of their bodies rather than their souls or minds seeking development, the entity grew in grace, in knowledge, in understanding.

And in the present those abilities arise from its desire, from its hopes to put into the word of the *day*, the experience of the day, in all phases of human experience, *lessons*—yea, symbols, yea tenets—that will drive as it were *home*, in those periods when the soul takes thought and counsel with itself, as to whence the experiences of the day are leading—as to whether they are leading to those activities that are the fruits of the spirit of truth and life, or to those that make for selfishness, and the aggrandizement of material appetites without thought of those things that are creative and only make the pure growths within the experience of others.

Hence whether it be in jest, in stories, in song or poem, or whether in skits that may show the home life, the lover—yea, the weary traveler yea the high-minded, and they that think better of themselves then they ought to think—*these* abilities are there. Use them. For He, even as then, will bless thee with His presence in same. And what greater assurance can there be in the experience of any soul than to know that He—yea, the Son of Mary—yea, the Son of the Father, the Maker of heaven and earth, the Giver of all good gifts—will be thy right hand, yea thy heart, thy mind, thy eye, thy heart itself—if ye will hold fast to Him!

Before that we find the entity was in the Egyptian land, during those periods when there were the gatherings of those from the turmoils, from the banishments, and those from the Atlantean land.

The entity then was among those from the lands that were later called the Parthenian lands, or what ye know as the Persian land from which the conquerors then of Egypt had come.

As a Princess from that land the entity came to study the mysteries for the service it might give to those of her own land, the Carpathians or as has been given, the entity was among the *first* of the pure white from that land to seek from the Priest and those activities in the Temple Beautiful for the purifying of self that she, too, might give to her own not only the tenets but the practical application of that which would bring home in the material experience an *assurance* in the separations from the body.

Thus in the abilities of the entity from that experience, as well as those gained throughout those activities, we find in the present: Just meting out day by day those visions, that ye have gained here, that ye have seen in thy experiences, thy sojourns, ye will find that *He* the keeper, *He* the Creator, will give the increase necessary for the activities in every sphere of thy experience.

For keeping inviolate that thou knowest gives assurance not only in self but in the promises that He will bear thee *up!*

If there is kept that purpose in self, there is little need for a return; save as one that may lead the way to those that are still in darkness.

As to the practical application, then:

In the writing, in the song; in the meting it out in the conversation day by day. For *ye* can only be the sower. *God* giveth the increase!

Faint not at well-doing.

Ready for questions.

Q: How can I extend the borders of my consciousness to include fourth dimen-

sional knowledge and achieve greater spiritual illumination?

A: These illuminations, the greater visions, only come by the communion with the true life and light from within.

For as thy body is the temple of thy *own* self, so is the kingdom of heaven within, even as He gave. And if ye will but open the door of thy consciousness and let Him come in, He will sup with thee and give thee that thou may *use* day by day.

Q: Where, when and what was my relationship to the entity now known as [1470], in any past incarnation, and what does he mean to my present life pattern?

A: In the Palestine period the self was as Judy, the entity [1470] was as the Roman that made light much, and later came to seek.

And thus in authority in self doth he find that those activities in the present will become much in the same way and manner. For not as one dependent upon the other, but one as bolstering as it were the purposes that may be held aright.

Q: Where, when and what was my past relationship to the entity now known as [1151], and what is the purpose of my present association with him?

A: In the same land.

Here we find quite a variation in the activity. For as the entity that walked in the way to Emmaus *found* that those records of those activities became part and parcel of the experience, so is that bond of sympathy found in the associations that awakens the urge for a *helpfulness without question* as one to another.

Q: Is radio the field in which I can best use my spiritual enlightenment and writing ability for the greatest service to the world?

A: Radio is a means of expression; writing is a means of confirmation and is longer *lasting.*

Q: Why do I get so little love, consideration and appreciation from those to whom I pour out the most service and devotion?

A: Study that which has been given thee relative to such, and ye will see that it is patience ye must learn, that ye must add to those virtues that have made thee ever the burden bearer for the many throughout those periods when the awakenings were coming.

Faint not because of thy loneliness, for who can be alone with His love, His promises abiding with thee!

These may make for a blooming into activity in thy experience, and *will*, if ye will give expression more and more to those promises that are thy very own.

For He, as He hath promised, may bring to thy remembrance *all* things—from the foundations of the earth. Know the Lord is nigh; and that those who keep watch, who keep faith *with* thee, are even as those of old—when there are the hundreds, yea the thousands that have never bended the knee to Baal, but as thee—only need that light, that assurance that He *is* the guiding light!

Q: How can I help my daughter, the entity now known as [. . .]?

A: Be not overanxious. Ever be ready rather to give an answer for the faith that lieth within. Not as argumentive, but as that which has been, which is, which ever will be the assurance to thee of the faith, the love that conquers all.

Q: Who and where is my real mate?

A: This may best be found by considering that as was the experience in those activities during the Palestine period, yea those full activities of the entity *as* Judy in that period with the Essenes. Study even that little which has been preserved of same. Ye will find him studying same also!

Q: Can you tell me anything of the activity and development of my son, the entity known in this life as [. . .] who died at the age of 13?

A: As has been given thee, let Him, the Way, the Life, reveal this to thee in thine *own* meditation. He is near at hand.

If thine eyes will be opened, if thy purposes will be set in the service, in the patience of love, He may reveal—as given—*all* things to thee.

Let thy deeper meditation be, in thine own way, but as these thoughts: *Lord, my Lord, my God! Thy handmaid seeks light and understanding! Open to my mind, my heart, my purpose, that which I may use in my daily service, my daily contacts, that will be more and more expressive of Thy love to the children of men.*

We are through for the present.

9. Case #5366

Editor's Note: In this next case, Cayce states that the entity whose name has been replaced with the number 5366, comes under no astrological influences and as for future earth incarnations he says "no such [incarnations] may be necessary in the experience again in the earth-materiality."

Text of Reading 5366-1 F 53
(Housewife, Protestant)

This Psychic Reading given by Edgar Cayce at the office of the Association, Arctic Crescent, Virginia Beach, Va., this 19th day of July, 1944, in accordance with request made by the self—Mrs. [5366], Associate Member of the Ass'n for Research & Enlightenment, Inc.

PRESENT

Edgar Cayce; Gertrude Cayce, Conductor; Gladys Davis, Jeanette Fitch, Stenos.

READING

Born October 31, 1890, on a farm near Bellefontaine, Ohio

Time of Reading Set bet. 3:30 to 4:30 P.M. Eastern War Time
. . . . , Mass.

GC: You will give the relations of this entity and the universe, and the universal forces; giving the conditions which are as personalities, latent and exhibited in the present life; also the former appearances in the earth plane, or giving time, place and the name, and that in each life which built or retarded the development for the entity; giving the abilities of the present entity, that to which it may attain, and how. You will answer the questions, as I ask them:

EC: My! Some very interesting characters have been born near Bellefontaine! This entity was among those with that one who persecuted the church so thoroughly and fiddled while Rome burned. That's the reason this entity in body has been disfigured by structural conditions. Yet may this entity be set apart. For through its experiences in the earth, it has advanced from a low degree to that which may not even necessitate a reincarnation in the earth. Not that it has reached perfection but there are realms for instruction if the entity will hold to that ideal of those whom it once scoffed at because of the pleasure materially brought in associations with those who did the persecuting.

In giving the interpretation, then, of the records of this entity, there is much that may be said but, as has been indicated, we would minimize the faults, and we would magnify the virtues. Thus may little or nothing be given that would deter the entity in any manner from holding fast to that purpose which has become that to which it may hold. For, as Joshua of old, the entity has determined (and sometimes the entity becomes very disturbed) "Others may do as they may, but as for me, I will serve the living God."

Astrological aspects would be nil in the experiences of the entity. (Let's pray with the entity.) No such may be necessary in the experience again in the earth-materiality. Remember, there are material urges and there are materials in other consciousnesses not three-dimensions alone.

As to the appearances in the earth, these would only be touched upon, as indicated, to be a helpful experience for the entity, as:

Before this we find the entity was in the land of the present nativity, through the experiences in seeking for new undertakings with the associates or companions. The entity became a helper to those who sought to know more of that which had been the prompting of individuals to seek freedom and to know that which is the spirit of creation or creative energies. Thus did the entity grow in attempting to interpret man's relationship to the Creative Forces or God. The name then was Jane Eyericson.

Before that we find the entity, as mentioned, was a companion or associate of that one [Nero] who persecuted those who believed in, those who accepted faith in righteousness, in goodness, in crucifying of body desires, in crucifying the emotions which would gratify only appetites of a body, either through the physical self or through physical appetites of gormandizing, and of material desire for the arousing more of the beast in individual souls.

In the experience, then, the entity is meeting self in that which was a part of the experience as Emersen.

Before that we find the entity was in the land when the children of promise entered into the promised land, when there were those whose companion or who father [Achan] sought for the gratifying of selfish desires in gold and garments and in things which would gratify only the eye. The entity was young in years and yet felt, as from those things which were told the entity, that a lack of material consideration was given the parent. The name then was Suthers.

Before that we find the entity was in the Egyptian land. The entity was among those who were trained in the Temple Beautiful for a service among its fellow men, contributing much to the household and the establishing of homes. Thus is the home near and dear to the entity, as are members of same, whether of the body-family or of the help or kinsmen.

Thus again may the entity find, in its application of those tenets and truths in the present, that answering in experiences of the entity in that land.

Then the entity was called Is-it-el.

As to the abilities:

Who would tell the rose how to be beautiful; who would give to the morning sun, glory; who would tell the stars how to be beautiful? Keep that faith! which has prompted thee. Many will gain much from thy patience, thy consistence, thy brotherly love.

Ready for questions.

Q: What locality is best for me?

A: In the middle west.

Q: What has been the incentive to heal and help others?

A: Read just what has been given.

Q: Should we invest a small sum of money in Tung Oil or Ramie land in the south, or a log cabin on a mountain side on . . . 's farm at . . . , Conn., for future vacations?

A: No. Those in the west we would prepare, or Ohio, Indiana, or Iowa. These would be the better and there invest; whether in Illinois, in oil, yes; Iowa, a rest home, yes; in Ohio, farmland.

Q: How have I been associated in the past with my husband, [4921]?

A: In the experience before this there were associations in which each was an incentive or a helper, and yet never closely associated. That's why ye disagree at times in the present. In the experience in Egypt in the same association as in the present, as were the children, though there were many more of them there.

Q: My son, [5249]?

A: As indicated.

Q: My son, [5242]?

A: As indicated.

Q: How can I best help them in the present?

A: In helping them to study to show themselves approved unto God, workmen not ashamed, rightly stressing the words of truth and keeping self unspotted from the world.

We are through with this reading.

10. Case #1741

Editor's Note: "The entity may so apply those tenets as have been set before self, in its ministration to those that are about the entity, that no return would be necessary in *this* experience or plane." Cayce emphasis on 'this" gives one the impression that 1741 may have some necessary experiences in other planes of life — a concept that Cayce's readings often presented to us, despite our earth focus.

Text of Reading 1741-1 F 42
(Governess in Jewish Family)

This Psychic Reading given by Edgar Cayce at his office, 115 West 35th Street, Virginia Beach, Va., this 15th day of October, 1930, in accordance with request made the by the self— Miss [1741], via her employers, Mr. [1734] and Mrs. [1732].

PRESENT

Edgar Cayce; Gertrude Cayce, Conductor; Gladys Davis, Steno. L. B. and Hugh Lynn Cayce.

READING

Born February 3, 1888, Sargans, Switzerland.

Time of Reading 11:40 A.M. Eastern Standard Time. New York City.

(Life Reading Suggestion)

EC: Yes, we have the entity and those relations with the universe and universal forces, as are latent and exhibited in the present entity, [1741].

In entering the present experience, we have the entity coming under the influence of Uranus and Venus, Jupiter and Mercury. Hence those conditions as personalities, manifestedly builded in the present entity:

One high minded, yet the tempered thought and experience influenced by those of an occult or mystic nature; love ruling in the influ-ences of the entity, and in the scope of mental abilities these take—especially interest—are influenced by those of the love's influence, rather than of *material* conditions, yet material forces are apparent in the influ-ences that bring such changes in the experience of the entity, as has made for that as builds for patience, long suffering, kindness, endur-ance, tolerance and brotherly love, faith, hope, charity to all. These are as the children of the entity's development, making for those influences as build in the present experience, as develops—which, when grown and manifested in the material actions of the body, bring that pleasing, patient personality as is manifested—especially with those whom the entity *would* influence; using then those armors that are rather of the nature of disarming to those that would be in a hurry, in a bluster. Not that wrath does not present itself, but rather that the influences through the *experiences* has brought that as develops the control, rather than be-ing controlled by such for the entity.

One appreciative of literature, especially those of the descriptive na-ture of the outdoors and the influence that same has upon those that experience—either in reading or in actuality—such visions, such sur-roundings, such scenes. Patient in that of study, especially as bear an influence towards those things that bespeak of the spiritual life. While in the entity's development there are set rules for self, tolerance in oth-ers brings a *beauty* to the entity's speech and activity that draws—rather than repels—the influence of the entity. In the appreciativeness of kindnesses, soft words, gentleness, the entity may be called one as ex-cels; making friends easily, enemies seldom; holding little grudges, yet *positive* in its ideals, in its ideas as to the approach to ideals.

One that is handy, or a handmaid in the arts of sewing, mending, or gathering together of the studies of such, and especially as brocades or laces, figures in cloth, interest the entity.

In the development, or that to which it may attain in the present, rather the application of that as has been set before self—for *well* has the way been chosen. Many depend *physically* upon, depend *mentally* upon, the activities of the entity. Be true to the duties set by self. Know that the way made is in keeping with the ideal set before self.

In appearances and the influences in the present experience:

In the one before this we find the entity among those who sat by the river, as the gatherings on the feast days, and listened to the speech and the exhortation by those who gave a new message from the foreign land to the women of Thyatira and Sidon, for the entity was then a seller of lace, purple brocade and linens, and in the *city* as of Lystra did the entity dwell—a maiden throughout the experience, and the entity gained through this experience, for much as was gained in the service set—and in the applications of the new rule or ideal as was given in this experience—did the entity apply and use in that experience. In the name Lystia. In the present, that of the aide, the teacher, the succor, the minister to the needs, the wants, of those dependent upon the activities of another, does the entity seek to find expression in that held within self's own heart.

In the one before this we find in that land known as the Egyptian land, and in the days when there were the incoming of the peoples from the hill country did the entity attempt to cause those in authority to rebel; yet in the changes as were wrought—for the entity was then among those of the royalty of that period or land, in the household of the ruler in the southern portion of the land—the entity lost and gained through the experience; being then in that place that gave *to* the land a teacher, through the body that afterward became a mighty one in word, in deed, and in activity. In the name Io-Li. In the present experience this gives the entity that ability to control self, even when those conditions that are held as imperative are overridden by others in position, power or place.

In the one before this we find in the land known as the Poseidan, or a portion of the old Atlantean. In this period the entity found much of those that pertained to the mysteries of nature, in the application of unseen forces, in the usages of same for man's indwelling, and man's physical dwelling. Hence much that is of the mystic, symbol, symbolistic, or of that as brings to the varied consciousnesses of an entity, does the entity often dwell upon; being mindful that those that are of the chemical, or chemical combines in the present, does not gain a hold that may not easily be set aside. In the name Ameer.

In the abilities of the entity in the present, as given, these may be made to excel—and the entity may so apply those tenets as have been set before self, in its ministration to those that are about the entity, that no return would be necessary in *this* experience or plane; for in *Him* is the light, and the light came among men, showing men the way to find that consciousness in *self*—for the *kingdom* is of *within*, and when self is made one *with* those forces there may be the accord as is necessary for "Come up higher. Being faithful over a few things, I will make thee ruler over many".

We are through.

Part 2

Karma

5

●

Edgar Cayce's Discourses on Karma

Reading 440-5

Well that karma be understood, and how it is to be met. For, in various thought—whether considered philosophy or religion, or whether from the more scientific manner of cause and effect—karma is all of these and more.

Rather it may be likened unto a piece of food, whether fish or bread, taken into the system; it is assimilated by the organs of digestion, and then those elements that are gathered from same are, made into the forces that flow through the body, giving the strength and vitality to an animate object, or being, or body.

So, in experiences of a soul, in a body, in an experience in the earth. Its thoughts make for that upon which the soul feeds, as do the activities that are carried on from the thought of the period make for the ability, of retaining or maintaining the active force or active principle of the thought *through* the experience.

Then, the soul re-entering into a body under a different environ either makes for the expending of that it has made through the experience in the sojourn in a form that is called in some religions as destiny of the soul, in another philosophy that which has been builded must be met in some way or manner, or in the more scientific manner that a certain cause produces a certain effect.

Hence we see that karma is *all* of these and more. What more? Ever since the entering of spirit and soul into matter there has been a way of redemption for the soul, to make an association and a connection with the Creator, *through* the love *for* the Creator that is in its experience. Hence *this*, too, must be taken into consideration; that karma may mean the development *for self*—and must be met in that way and manner, or it may mean that which has been acted upon by the cleansing influences of the way and manner through which the soul, the mind-soul, or the soul-mind is purified, or to be purified, or purifies itself, and hence those changes come about—and some people term it "Lady Luck" or "The body is born under a lucky star." It's what the soul-mind has done *about* the source of redemption of the soul! Or it may be yet that of cause and effect, as related to the soul, the mind, the spirit, the body.

Reading 276–7

What has karma to do with this body, then? What is the fate, or the destiny, of such a soul? Has it already been determined as to what it may do, or be, for the very best? or has it been so set that the activities and the influences, the environs and the hereditary forces, are to alter?

These indeed are worthy questions, in the light of that which has been given.

If there be any virtue or truth in those things given in the spiritual or Christian or Jehovah-God faith, His laws are immutable. What laws are immutable, if truth and God Himself is a growing thing—yet an ever changeable, and yet "ever the same, yesterday and today and forever"?

These things, these words, to many minds become contradictory, but they are in their inception *not* contradictory; for Truth, Life, Light, Immortality, are only words that give expression to or convey a concept of one and the same thing.

Hence, Destiny is: "As ye sow, so shall ye reap." And like begets like! And the first law of nature, which is the material manifestation of spiritual law in a physical world, is self-propagation—which means that it seeks self- preservation and the activity of the same law that brought the thought of man (or the spirit of man) into existence—companionship!

What, then, is karma? And what is destiny? What has the soul done, in the spiritual, the material, the cosmic world or consciousness, respecting the knowledge or awareness of the laws being effective in his experience—whether in the earth, in the air, in heaven or in hell? These are ever one; for well has it been said, "Though I take the wings of the morning and fly unto the utmost parts of the heavens, Thou art there! Though I make my bed in hell, Thou art there! Though I go to the utmost parts of the earth, Thou art there! Truth, Life, God! Then, that which is cosmic—or destiny, or karma—depends upon what the soul has done about that it has become aware of.

What, you say, has this to do with this soul, this entity, that—as we have given—is well balanced and attuned as to that it will do; by its own activating forces of its will, its desire—that arise from its experiences in the mental, the spiritual and the material world? Because it is thus making its destiny, its karma! For, *He* will stand in the stead. For, by sin came death; by the shedding of blood came freedom—freedom from a consciousness, into a greater consciousness.

So, in His promises do we live and move and have our being. Be patient. But know much may be done.

Reading 311-7

Q: Have I much bad karma to work out in this life?

A: *Karma* is rarely understood, in "being *worked out*." There is, has been prepared, a way in which karma—as ordinarily known—may be forgiven thee. There are constantly those necessary temptations being presented before each soul, each individual, each developing force in God's own nature; that, are these left upon those Forces, or to those Forces rather than to self, there is *little* to be feared in that that would beset.

Editor's Note: This next reading was given for a Quaker teacher, which may explain that intensely Christ-centered directive to Mrs. [2067].

Reading 2067-2

Q: Considering my ideals, purposes and karmic pattern, as well as the conditions which I face at present, in what specific direction should I seek expression for my talents and abilities in order to render the greatest possible service?

A: This is rather a compound question, for it presumes or presupposes as to ideals, as to purposes, and as to self's concept of karma.

What *is* karma? and what *is* the pattern?

He alone is each soul pattern. He *alone* is each soul pattern! *He* is thy *karma*, if ye put thy trust *wholly* in Him! See?

Not that every soul shall not give account for the deeds done in the body, and in the body meet them! but in each meeting, in *each* activity, let the pattern—(not in self, not in mind alone, but in Him)—be the guide.

As to the outlet, as to the manner of expression—to give as to this or that is merely giving opinions. For, all must be quickened—there must be the quickening of the spirit.

As we find indicated in the expression of thought, by or through writing is *one* manner, or one channel. Another is by the speaking, the becoming as a lecturer, an interpreter for groups of various sects or forms of activity—whether psychological groups, Theosophist groups, Sunday School groups of various denominations, or of whatever cult. For, the ideal is to set those aright! not by dogmatic activity but by reasoning—as He—with others.

When questioned as to political, economic or social order, what were His answers? Did He condemn the man who was born blind? Did He condemn the woman taken in adultery? Did He condemn the man that was healed of palsy or of leprosy? Did He condemn any? Rather did He point out that in *Him* each meets that karmic condition found in self, and that the pattern is in Him; doing good, being kind, being patient, being loving in *every* experience of man's activity.

Do thou likewise.

Editor's Note: In this next reading we see Cayce's biblical foundation (both Old and New Testament) coming through in a mystical vision of the early Christian concept of the blood sacrifice. Cayce equates it with the removal of karma.

Reading 2828-5

When it was given "Whosoever sheddeth man's blood, by man shall his blood be shed." That is, in this case, the blood of his will, of this purpose, of this physical desire to carry on in his own ways of activity and by those conditions in the body itself being thwarted. The entity thwarted others and is meeting it in self. That is karma. In the blood of the Christ as was shed karma is met and then it becomes the law, not of cause and effect, but of being justified by faith in Him. Then, may we use, may we apply those things of the material earth *and* the spiritual combination to become again sons of God. Not sons of Belial or of the devil.

6

●

Examples of Karma in Edgar Cayce's Discourses

Text of Reading 275-19 F 18
(Student, Protestant)

This psychic reading given by Edgar Cayce at his office, 115 West 35th Street, Virginia Beach, Va., this 16th day of May, 1931, in accordance with request made by self—Miss [275].

Edgar Cayce; Gertrude Cayce, Conductor; Gladys Davis, Steno.

READING

Time of Reading . . . Ave., 11:25 A.M. Eastern Standard Time . . . . , N. Y.

GC: You will have before you the information in the life reading through these sources for [275] on October 13, 1930. You will now give the place, time, description of life, with its resultant karma in entity's incarnation as Partheniasi. You will answer the questions which will be asked concerning these.

EC: Yes, we have the information as given relative to the entity's sojourn in the earth's plane as Partheniasi.

As we find, the record as is *builded* by an entity in the akashian record is to the mental world as the cinema is to the material or physical world, as pictured in its activity. So, in the direction to an entity and its entrance into the material plane in a given period, time, place—which indicate the relative position of the entity as related to the universe or to the universal sources—then one only turns, as it were, to those *records* in the akashian forms to read that period of that builded or that lost during *that* experience.

In this entity's experience and the karma builded, or that to be met in the various experiences of the entity:

During the period in Nero's reign in Rome, in the latter portion of same, the entity was then in the household of Parthesias—and one in whose company many became followers of, adherents to, those called Christians in the period, and during those persecutions in the arena when there were physical combats. The entity was as a spectator of such combats, and under the influence of those who made light of them; though the entity felt in self that there was more to that held by such individuals, as exhibited in the arena, but the entity—to carry that that was held as necessary with the companionship of those about same— laughed at the injury received by one of the girls [301] [GD's note: [301] is now her brother [282]'s wife, living in the same household and helping to nurse [275] in the arena, and *suffered* in *mental anguish* when she saw later—or became cognizant of—the physical suffering brought to the body *of* that individual during the rest of the sojourn. The suffering that was brought was of a *mental* nature, and when music—especially of the lyre, harp, or of the zither—was played, the entity *suffered* most; for the song and the music that was played during that experience brought—as it were—the experience to the entity. Hence in meeting same in the present, there has been builded that which the entity passes through, or "under the rod"—as it were—of that as of being pitied, laughed at, scorned, for the inability of the personal body to partake of those in the material activities as require the need of all of the physical body; yet in the music, in the acceptance, in the building of those forces through that which laughed at, which scorned—though knowing; now *knowing*, laugh to scorn those who would *doubt* the activities of the forces that build in a material body that activity in every cell, every force, to make a perfect body. Ready for questions.

Q: Give exact guidance how entity can best make good her karma during this life.

A: As has been outlined, that—now knowing that as is to be met, no scorn, no sneer, but with patience, with fortitude, with praise, with the giving of pleasure in music, in kindnesses, in gentle words, in bespeaking of that as may build for a perfect mind, a perfect soul, a perfect body, may the entity overcome those things that have beset—that not often understood, those things that so easily beset us; making the will one with the Creator and the Creative Forces. Be used by *them*, and the channel—the cup will run over with blessings. Those things that easily beset bespeak not of those only that are weaknesses in the flesh; but the weaknesses in the *flesh* are the scars of the soul! and these, only in that of making the will one with His, being washed—as it were in the blood of the lamb. We are through.

Reading 538-30

GC: You will have before you the body and the enquiring mind of [538]. You will give a detailed life-history of this entity's appearance in Egypt as Isris, and of her association with those of that period with whom she is closely associated in the present. You will answer the questions which will be asked regarding this, and also regarding information which has been given her through these sources and her present development.

EC: Yes, we have that record as made in *that* experience. In the entering as a record, in the household of him raised to the position of priest enduring the banishment of the entity with others, becoming a favorite of the king, in the household of the king, and a dancer in the temple service; becoming one favored by the priest, and with the associations became a mother in the king's household, banished with priest to the Nubian land; in exile for nine years, returned with those of the exile and those gathered about the priest and *his* associates. Many were the associations directly, indirectly, of the entity during this period. Beautiful of body and figure, many are the casts that were made during the period as an aide or dancer in temple service. In the latter days more active in the issuing forth of those tenets as were carried to the various groups or peoples, as the *kingdom* extended its appeal to other lands. Ready for questions.

Q: What karma does the entity bring to the present from this period, and how may I work this out?

A: Easily holding grudges where there are misunderstandings, or those who apparently injure the body in thought or deed. In working same out, this becomes necessary—as we find in answering such questions—that we turn entirely away from that as is a record and use either that as the *ideal* as has been builded, or was builded in that period and later became manifest through those forces as were known in the Son.* In overcoming karma, or that innate influence that arises from experience of the soul in its passage through material planes, the meeting of individuals, entities, drawn to or from by innate urges that become impelling in many ways, these are acted upon by that as is builded by an entity as its ideal. Well to learn that lesson! for as is builded, then does the comparison come when the soul passes from experience to experience by that it has held as its standard. This becomes confusing to the body, as we view from this plane. This, then: As one builds in self that ideal as takes away the errors of material things, as this grows, so does the soul become more like Him—see?

Q: How may I better fit myself to aid in this work, which is so influenced by this Egyptian period?

A: In drawing nearer and nearer to that *mind* as was *in* Him who *crystallized* the *experiences* of the period in the earth ten thousand five hundred years later. As this becomes understood, may each soul, each entity, apply those truths as given, then as crystallized, as exemplified, as made one in Him; so may a soul, meditating in those tenets, come to know how, what manner, self may apply self's abilities in daily contacts with individuals, bring forth that as makes for the better, the clarifying, the exemplifying, of those laws, loves, truths.

Reading 2842-2

Q: Please tell me what my karma is, in order that I may strive to overcome it.

A: Overcome that fear and dread in self. That is the karma. That is that to be conquered in self, for this applies to the entity in its secular, physical, mental, and spiritual body—for, as is seen, when the body

physical, mental or spiritual has set self to disregard fear of conse-
quences, so long as that activity was in keeping with the first law of the
directed or creative energy, all well! but when applied in the manner of
I! the vibration has brought that as of against the stone wall.

Q: Why have I always had more or less of an aversion to the opposite sex?

A: Rather that of the complex, brought on by fear—as has been
given—in the various experiences of the entity in and through the
earth's plane. This at times as the entity has felt mentally, and at other
times felt inwardly has been detrimental, yet—would that law become
the fullness of the truth in the entity—let that prayer be: I will be all
things unto all peoples, that I may *gain* the more. *Not* in the sense of
building in self as one that would live upon the efforts of another, but
that—being all things—I may be understood, and may *understand* the
viewpoint, the concept, the impelling force, the reflective angle to which
another sees its God.

*Q: Have I a right to demand abundance, or should I be content with my small
income?*

A: Be *content* with what thou hast, but never be *satisfied* with what
thou hast. Abundance is the lot of him who is in accord with those
truths of the Creative Energy, just as the world—the hills, the cattle, the
gold—is mine, sayeth the Lord. I will repay, sayeth the Lord. Put thine
self in that attitude, that position, of reflecting that as is of the Creative
Energy, and that necessary—and over an abundance will be in thine
hand.

Reading 262–57 (early deaths)

*Q: Does the truth, "By becoming aware in a material world was the only manner
through which spiritual forces might become aware of their separation from spiritual
surroundings" show that the reincarnation of those who die in childhood is necessary?*

A: As the awareness comes by separation (which is being manifested
in materiality as we know it in the present), there is the necessity of the
sojourning in *each* experience for the developments of the influences
necessary in each soul's environ, each soul's attributes, to become again
aware of being in the *presence* of the Father. Hence the reincarnation into
this or that influence, and those that are only aware of material or car-

nal influences for a moment may be as *greatly* impressed as were a finite mind for a moment in the presence of Infinity. How long was the experience of Saul in the way to Damascus? How long was the experience of Stephen as he saw the Master standing—not sitting, *standing*? How long was the experience of those that saw the vision that beckoned to them, or any such experience?

When one considers the birth of a soul into the earth, the more often is the body and the body-mind considered than the soul—that is full-grown in a breath. For, did the Father (or Infinity) bring the earth, the worlds into existence, how much greater is a day in the house of the Lord—or a moment in His presence—than a thousand years in carnal forces?

Hence a soul even for a flash, or for a breath, has perhaps experienced even as much as Saul [later, Paul] in the way [to Damascus].

7

●

Edgar Cayce's Tips for Meeting Karma

Reading 2271-1

Q: What karma do I have to overcome in order to free myself mentally and spiritually?

A: *Karma* is rather the lack of living to that *known* to do! As ye would be forgiven, so forgive in others. *That* is the manner to meet karma.

Reading 2990-2

Q: Please explain karma to me in relation to my eye condition, and how it may best be met in the present?

A: Read that just given, and as to how you may apply it. Karma is met either in self or in Him. For, as has been given, "in the day ye eat thereof—or in the day ye entertain fear, the day ye entertain sin—the soul must die." Not in that moment, possibly not in that era, but if the soul continues in sin, that is karma, that is cause and effect. But God has not willed that any soul should perish; He has with every temptation prepared a way of escape.

Hence, He, the Word, the Light, the Truth, came into the earth, paid the price of death, that we through Him might have life more abundantly; eternal life, the consciousness of eternal life; the consciousness of eternity; and that we are one with Him.

Editor's Note: This next reading reveals how karma does not have to become an actual physical experience, but be met in the mental and spiritual consciousness.

Reading 1635-3

Before this the entity was in the household of the Audubons. There the entity was the daughter of its present mother, and not too long-lived in that experience. For, the entity then was destroyed—or met sudden death—in an accident, in a car, or a horse and car.

These are latent conditions in the present experience for the entity, then; and warnings must be entertained and kept, not as to keeping the entity from such, but *know* with whom any traveling is done—else there may be accidents in car or in travel that may make of the body a partial invalid. These are a part of the karma, unless there is kept that law of grace through which karma is *not* an actual experience.

Hence there shall be great stress in the unfoldment or development of the entity, upon its trust in *divine* sources, of its care, of its intent, of its *trust* in those with whom it becomes active—not as to *daring*, but as for purpose, as for hope, as for those forces of the divine nature; that the entity in its intent and purpose may be kept in a sound, perfect body to better fulfill its purpose in the earth in its present sojourn.

Editor's Note: In some cases, Cayce chose not to address the karma but to simply get beyond it, as in this next reading for a young woman.

Reading 2072-14

Q: What is the karmic cause of the physical condition of this body?

A: This would have to do with other influences. Let's leave karma out. For there is a way, and the trust is in the divine within that may be in attune with the infinite. The karma—well, these would be sad. Leave this out. Just change it.

Q: How can one be sure that a decision is in accordance with God's will?

A: As indicated here before. Ask self in the own conscious self, "Shall I do this or not?" The voice will answer within. Then meditate, ask the same, Yes or No. You may be very sure if thine own conscious self and the divine self is in accord, you are truly in that activity indicated, "My spirit beareth witness with thy spirit." You can't get far wrong in following the word, as ye call the word of God.

8

●

From Karma to Grace

Reading 2800-2

Yet, it is a fact that a life experience is a manifestation of divinity. And the mind of an entity is the builder. Then as the entity sets itself to do or to accomplish that which is of a creative influence or force, it comes under the interpretation of the law between karma and grace. No longer is the entity then under the law of cause and effect—or karma, but rather in grace it may go on to the higher calling as set in Him.

Keep the faith in the Lord, not in things. Some of those activities in the present may tend to lead the mind astray, for it to become a disciple of an idea rather than of ideals. But let thy purpose be in the Lord, and thy ways may be pleasing to Him.

Reading 3177-1

Q: *What is the karma which follows me?*

A: This—find it in self. Know, so long as we feel there is karma, it is cause and effect. But in righteousness we may be justified before the Throne; thus we may pass from cause and effect, or karma, to that of grace.

This is the attitude; not of self-righteousness no, but of blessed assurance that He is able to take all that we may commit unto Him against any experience in our lives.

Reading 2981-1

In giving an interpretation of the records as we find them, there is much from which to choose. These we would choose with the desire and purpose that this may be a helpful experience for the entity; enabling the entity to better fulfill those purposes for which it entered this present sojourn.

Much that would be of interest might be gained by some, as to why the entity entered this present sojourn; partly by choice of self. For, viewed from the spirit, much of time and space in a material concept loses its relationship—and becomes *now*.

Hence those experiences which have brought distortions in the material plane are not merely because of karmic law, but the application of karmic law in the life of the individual entity.

Thus we find those greater opportunities for the entity meeting same, not only in the law of cause and effect—or karma—but also in the application of the law of grace.

The activities of the entity, thusly, are tied in the material, in the mental, in the spiritual, with what the entity does about the choices made.

The body of each entity is the temple of the living God. There He has promised to meet the entity. To live, to be—and that activity—unto the glory of the Creative Forces is the purpose of the entrance of each entity into material consciousness.

That met, that accomplished in any experience, is unto that unfoldment of the awareness of the oneness of self with that Creative Force which it, the entity, would magnify.

Many influences enter in the experience of this entity; more from activities in the material plane than from what might be ordinarily termed the astrological sojourns. While the sojourns of the entity in those consciousnesses we term the astrological aspects do have their influence, these are manifested more in the manner or way of thinking; as indicated in Mercury, Venus, Jupiter and Saturn.

These, then, bring the high mental abilities; the interest in music, art, and the universal consciousness—also the affliction in Saturn. Thus the desire of change in the activities. Thus the necessity, as in most entities, that patience be practiced, not only as a theory but as a reality in the experience; not only patience with things, conditions (that are a part of the experience), but with people, with others, with time, with influences that may alter the activities of the entity.

Reading 2727-1

While the astrological influences are apparent, we find that these do not in this particular case run true to the ordinarily termed astrological effects; varying because of the application the entity has made in those relationships. Just as that influence termed by some students as karma. This is the natural law, yes. But there *is* the law of grace, of mercy. And this is *just* as applicable as the law of karma, dependent upon the stress or the emphasis put upon varied things.

Reading 3249-1

Q: Are these ailments karma, if so what did I do and how can I wash them out?

A: These are part karma and part just self. Karmic conditions, of course, are cause and effect. There is grace through the power of the belief of the entity in the divine, in His materialization, His manifestation and His glorification. Then the purpose of the entity should be ever to use whatever may be the abilities to glorify and magnify Him in the earth.

Q: Is my soul going ahead or have I missed the call of this incarnation?

A: Ever going ahead. Though it may appear at times to fail, there is nothing that can separate thee from the love and the knowledge of the Father save self.

Q: What do I do that is wrong?

A: Who made us a judge over thee or anyone else? What are thy ideals? Parallel thy activities with thine ideals, not merely in mind but put it on paper so that you may study and take a lesson from same.

Q: What should I do to further my advancement on the path?

A: Study to show thyself approved unto God, a workman not ashamed; rightly dividing the words of truth, keeping self unspotted from condemnation of others or of things.

Reading 2746-2

The entity was an Atlantean, as indicated. This experience was indicated because there had been the opportunity in self, in which there was the use of spiritual ideals for self-indulgence. Hence such entities, in each period of activity in the material plane, will either make reparations or—rather should it be said—turn to the law of grace instead of the law of karma, and will come out of the experience as a wonderful success or a miserable failure. They are extremes, just as the entity itself has found in the present. There are periods when there is the decision that something is desirable and you don't stop until you have it! These are extremes. Time and space and patience are most needed oft, that few souls or individuals are willing to pay the price for—until they grow to be such, you see.

Just as has so oft been indicated, one doesn't fall out of a tree into heaven, or an airplane, or fly into heaven, but one grows in grace, in knowledge, in understanding, in perfecting within self those applications of tenets and truths that bring to the activities the spiritual, the mental growth.

Reading 2987-1

The name then was Eloise White. Yet the entity in the latter portion of its experience gained, for it came in contact with some of those who had suffered through the destruction of those lands now called Chicago or Dearborn. These brought a stabilizing of self, in the understanding that with what measure ye mete it is measured to thee again. It is the law of cause and effect, and is thus called karma. It is also the law of grace, of mercy, for if ye would have mercy ye must show mercy. If ye would have peace it must be first within self, and ye must be peaceful and create peace wherever you go, with whomever ye contact, and not dissension.

In the latter portion of that sojourn the entity helped others, by teachings; as ye may in the present, in the application of lessons of truth, gems of knowledge as may be in the soul experiences of the entity; and the application of same may bring harmony in the experience.

Reading 3243-1

As we find, conditions here are karmic. And unless the body would accept the responsibility of the general condition for self, then go about to correct same through the law, not of karma but of grace—not a great deal may be done.

Reading 5209-1

The karmic conditions are needed for the entity, or soul development of the entity, and those who have the responsibility of same; in that source from which all healing comes. For whether it be medicinal, mechanical or what sources, healing can only come from the divine. For as has been indicated, "Who healeth all thy diseases?" Him in whom we live and move and have our being.

Thus we may through those administrations of that which is the spirit of truth made manifest, turn this karma, or law, to grace and mercy. For the pattern hath been given those who seek to know His face.

Reading 1648-2

As has been indicated through these channels, there is never a chance meeting, or any association, that hasn't its meaning or purpose in the development of an individual entity or soul.

Then, as we have indicated, if any entity, any individual, takes a meeting, any association, with the purpose or the desire to use same for self-indulgence, self-aggrandizement, and no thought of the purposes of any activity through the development of the soul for its purpose as it enters, then it becomes that as may be or is called *karma*—or the individual becomes subject to *law*!

And, as has been pronounced, the letter of the law killeth, but the spirit of the law maketh alive.

Then the spirit of the law is exemplified in He that *is* the Law of Love, and Grace, and Mercy, and Truth.

And they that use such associations, such meetings as such, become helpmeets one to another—or stepping-stones for a greater development.

Who Was Edgar Cayce?
Twentieth Century Psychic and Medical Clairvoyant

Edgar Cayce (pronounced Kay-Cee, 1877-1945) has been called the "sleeping prophet," the "father of holistic medicine," and the most-documented psychic of the 20th century. For more than 40 years of his adult life, Cayce gave psychic "readings" to thousands of seekers while in an unconscious state, diagnosing illnesses and revealing lives lived in the past and prophecies yet to come. But who, exactly, was Edgar Cayce?

Cayce was born on a farm in Hopkinsville, Kentucky, in 1877, and his psychic abilities began to appear as early as his childhood. He was able to see and talk to his late grandfather's spirit, and often played with "imaginary friends" whom he said were spirits on the other side. He also displayed an uncanny ability to memorize the pages of a book simply by sleeping on it. These gifts labeled the young Cayce as strange, but all Cayce really wanted was to help others, especially children.

Later in life, Cayce would find that he had the ability to put himself into a sleep-like state by lying down on a couch, closing his eyes, and folding his hands over his stomach. In this state of relaxation and meditation, he was able to place his mind in contact with all time and space—the universal consciousness, also known as the super-conscious mind. From there, he could respond to questions as broad as, "What are the secrets of the universe?" and "What is my purpose in life?" to as specific as, "What can I do to help my arthritis?" and "How were the pyramids of Egypt built?" His responses to these questions came to be called "readings," and their insights offer practical help and advice to individuals even today.

The majority of Edgar Cayce's readings deal with holistic health and the treatment of illness. Yet, although best known for this material, the sleeping Cayce did not seem to be limited to concerns about the physical body. In fact, in their entirety, the readings discuss an astonishing 10,000 different topics. This vast array of subject matter can be narrowed down into a smaller group of topics that, when compiled together, deal with the following five categories: (1) Health-Related Information; (2) Philosophy and Reincarnation; (3) Dreams and Dream Interpretation; (4) ESP and Psychic Phenomena; and (5) Spiritual Growth, Meditation, and Prayer.

Learn more at EdgarCayce.org.

What Is A.R.E.?

Edgar Cayce founded the non-profit Association for Research and Enlightenment, Inc. (A.R.E.®) in 1931, to explore spirituality, holistic health, intuition, dream interpretation, psychic development, reincarnation, and ancient mysteries—all subjects that frequently came up in the more than 14,000 documented psychic readings given by Cayce.

The Mission of the A.R.E. is to help people transform their lives for the better, through research, education, and application of core concepts found in the Edgar Cayce readings and kindred materials that seek to manifest the love of God and all people and promote the purposefulness of life, the oneness of God, the spiritual nature of humankind, and the connection of body, mind, and spirit.

With an international headquarters in Virginia Beach, Va., regional representatives throughout the U.S., Edgar Cayce Centers in more than thirty countries, and individual members in more than seventy countries, the A.R.E. community is a global network of individuals.

A.R.E. conferences, international tours, camps for children and adults, regional activities, and study groups allow like-minded people to gather for educational and fellowship opportunities worldwide.

A.R.E. offers membership benefits and services that include a quarterly body-mind-spirit member magazine, *Venture Inward,* a member newsletter covering the major topics of the readings, and access to the entire set of readings in an exclusive online database.

Learn more at EdgarCayce.org.